799.2 NOB
Nobel, Dodman J.
   Whitetail hunter
education

AVON BRANCH LIBRARY
BOX 977 / 0280 BEAVER ___ ___
AVON, CO 81620 949-6797

WHITETAIL HUNTER EDUCATION

by

Dodman J. Nobel

To Mary Jane, my wife, partner and best friend. She celebrates my victories while understanding and comforting my hunting failures. Her unselfish attitude toward hunting is the greatest blessing that a hunter could have and it is certainly appreciated.

FIRST EDITION

Copyright 1995, by Dodman J. Nobel
Library of Congress Catalog Card No: 94-90454
ISBN: 1-56002-489-5

UNIVERSITY EDITIONS, Inc.
59 Oak Lane, Spring Valley
Huntington, West Virginia 25704

INTRODUCTION

On November 30, 1990, the author, Dodman "Dod" Jay Nobel, turned 50 years old and shot deer number 50. This *Whitetail Hunter Education* book contains information valuable to the hunter, both for the sake of success and in the interest of propagating the sport of hunting. The value of this book translates into over 40 years of hunting experience mixed with classroom preparation for Hunter Education classes, written into individual chapters that took months to research and hours to write but that can be read by a whitetail hunter in only a few minutes per chapter. Information relative to whitetail deer hunting is generously shared, hunting miscalculations admitted and successful strategy documented. These writings are intended to entertain and educate gun and bow hunters, both beginners and veterans. Technical data mixed with hunting philosophies and stories describe how-to procedures in an enlightened fashion. For all who have the opportunity to read this book, *Good hunting to you!*

Motivation

WHY I HUNT!

There is an intimate need in me to return to the wilds. Hunting is intoxicating. It is fed by companioning wild animals while I hunt, and nourished by inhaling nature. In a few short generations we have left our wilderness ancestors behind and succumbed to civilization. Part of us, the part that craves the wilds, still loves and clings to the simple life and freedoms of the past. We envy the pioneers and their woodsman talents that formed our roots. We envision them as we pursue deer with our modern-primitive equipment of bow or muzzleloading rifle. We have the best of both worlds as we combine with society for our comforts and escape to the woods for our achievements.

Although hunting is only a fraction of our heritage, for some of us it is a main stream bloodline. Hunting is more than just a sport, it is a science. A whitetail hunter that loves deer may seem like a paradox to some, but to me it is a categorical truth. I hunt because I am a hunter.
—D.J.N.
November 30, 1994

Photo by Ted Rose

CONTENTS

TRACKS AND FACTS - Deer tracks, antler development and other whitetail data, 5

SURVIVAL BY SENSES - Discussion of the acute whitetail senses, 13

WHITETAIL FALL FEEDING HABITS - The key to hunting is to locate the feeding areas, 17

THE PATH OF LEAST RESISTANCE - Deer will find the easiest route if undisturbed, 21

LET THE WEATHER HELP CUT THE NOTCHES IN YOUR DEER LICENSE - How the weather affects deer behavior and hunting methods, 25

DRIVE FOR KNOWLEDGE - Older method for hunting is good training for beginners, 27

HOW DO I HUNT THEE? LET ME COUNT THE WAYS - Stand, stillhunting, drive and float hunting, 31

ON THE TRAIL - Year around scouting goals, 36

O.D. SUCCESS - How to prepare for opening day, 41

BREAKING THE SILENCE - Rattling procedures, 46

DEER SOUNDS IN THE FOREST - Deer vocal sounds used for hunting, 50

THE BUCKS STOP HERE - Rub and scrape hunting procedures, 55

CAN TOXOPHILITES BE DANGEROUS TO YOUR HEALTH? - Archery tackle, bow tuning procedure, practice and hunting preparation, 63

GET HIGH TO HUNT WHITETAILS - Strategy for high bowhunting stand, 70

DOE SCENT DIVERSION - Bow hunting strategy using doe urine, 74

SMOKEPOLES AND OTHER HUNTING ARMS - Description of arms and ammunition used to hunt whitetail deer, 77

THE BEST TIME TO SQUEEZE THE TRIGGER - Know your limits and practice the correct way, 82

TREESTANDS I HAVE KNOWN - The best location to set treestands, 86

THE SECOND HUNT - Skills of tracking wounded animals, 94

WANTED: A FEW GOOD HUNTERS - Pertinent factors that hunters should be aware of to help insure and promote the sport of hunting, 98

ENJOYING THE HUNT - Allow yourself to enjoy being in the woods, 105

IS YOUR PHOTOGRAPH WORTHY OF YOUR TROPHY? - Ideas for posing pictures and recording hunting memories, 107

WILDERNESS VISIONS - Memories of wilderness views, 112

DEER CAMP SOCIETY - Special fraternal bonds and stories from deer camp, 115

THAT'S MY DEER! - Youngster cleverly identifies his deer, 119

PREPARE TO SURVIVE - Procedures to prevent getting lost, survival tactics and requirements to find lost hunters, 121

HUNTERS BEWARE! - First aid, hypothermia and lyme disease, 127

CLOTHES FOR THE HUNTER - Clothes from head to toes, 131

FINDING A NEEDLE IN A HAYSTACK - When and where to search for shed antlers, 137

CARING FOR YOUR DEER - Steps to protect your deer and provide the best venison, 139

BUTCHERING YOUR DEER - Step by step photos of home butchering, 142

VENISON HOME CANNING - How to can venison, 146

EXTENDING THE VENISON SEASON - Jerky, sausage and other venison recipes, 148

APPENDIX:

    How to Age Deer

    Deer Weight Formula

    Handgun Ballistics

    Rifle Ballistics

    B&C Scoresheet Typical

    B&C Scoresheet Non-Typical

    P&Y Score Requirements and entry form

    List of organizations and their stand on hunting

    Hunters Checklist

"One does not hunt in order to kill, one kills in order to have hunted."
José Ortega Y. Gasset
(1883-1955)
Spanish Philosopher

TRACKS AND FACTS

From the tracks they leave behind, to their individual scent, to the amazing antlers that create so much excitement, the whitetail deer is a fascinating game animal.

Distinguishing the tracks of a buck from a doe, even under ideal conditions, is difficult for most of us but the drawings from Buckmasters should help. Studying the clues left by a deer's tracks will help you learn about the deer in your area. Deer hooves are composed of keratin, the same as our toenails and fingernails. A dominant, mature buck will have a rounded hoof, worn from years of pawing for food and making autumn scrapes. Careful inspection will reveal that the deer's front hooves are usually larger than their hind. Notice, that as a young deer walks, its hind foot steps into the imprint of its fore foot.

The body size of a whitetail may vary from the smaller southern deer, having a shoulder height of 28" to the northern species standing at 40" to the top of the shoulder. Average live weights of these two extremes might range from 80 pounds to 180 pounds. According to Leonard Lee Rue III in his *Deer of North America*, the largest verified whitetail was a 402 pound field dressed deer killed during 1926 in Minnesota, with an estimated live weight of 511 pounds.

With moderate weather and good habitat, a mature doe will normally carry twins throughout her approximate 203 day gestation period. Female fawns can breed in December of their first year, usually bearing a single fawn. Results of research by Dr. James Kroll, deer biologist at Austin State University, Texas show that a mature doe with a scarcity of winter feed may have only one fawn instead of two. Extreme cases of starvation may result in both fawns dying and being re-absorbed back into the doe's system to promote her own survival.

Twins are common for well nourished doe. These two youngsters are 8-10 weeks old.

Deer Tracks

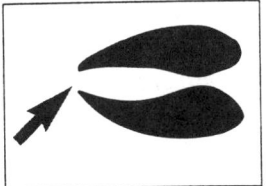

YOUNG DEER
The young deer typically have sharp, pointed hooves.

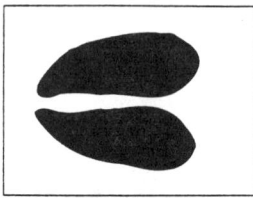

BUCK TRACK
A mature buck's tracks range from 2-3/4" to 3-1/2" in length.

BUCK AND DOE TRACKS
Rear tracks of young bucks and does slightly overlap their front tracks.

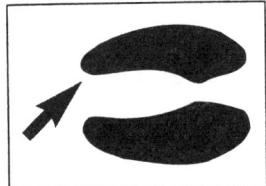

OLD DEER
Toes of older deer hooves are often worn and more rounded than those of younger deer.

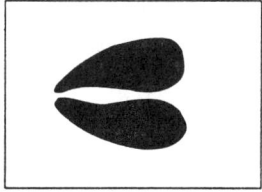

DOE TRACK
A mature doe track ranges from 2-1/4 to 2-3/4 inches in length.

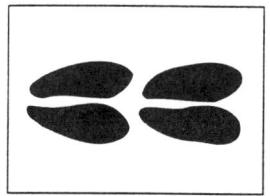

LARGE-BODIED BUCK
Rear tracks of a mature buck fall slightly behind their front tracks with no overlap.

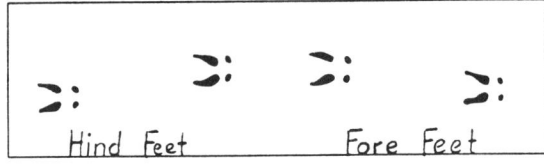

DEER RUNNING IN SOFT SOIL
A running deer, or a deer walking in very soft soil or mud will leave a splayed track with dew claw marks visible behind the hoof print.

A bounding deer will leave splayed hoof prints from 2-1/2 to 6 feet apart, and sometimes farther.

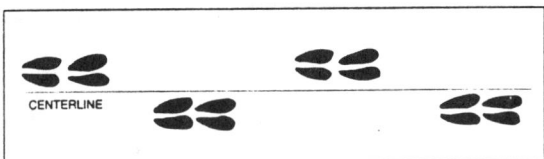

MATURE LARGE-BODIED BUCK
His tracks will be several inches apart in width, well to the right and left of a centerline. An old buck's front tracks may point slightly outward.

Buckmasters® Whitetail Magazine/Young Bucks®

WHITETAIL GLANDS

The glands of a deer perform a fingerprint identity in the whitetail community. The five main glands include: 1. tarsal (on the inner side of the hind legs at the hocks), 2. metatarsal (on the outside of the hind feet), 3. interdigital (between the lobes of the hoof), 4. pre-orbital (front corner of the eyes), and 5. forehead (at the antler base of bucks).

When one deer meets another, they smell the tarsal glands, similar to a dog checking another dog. Bucks will urinate over this gland into a scrape during the rut, resulting in darkened leg hairs and a distinctive aroma that can be detected at a distance.

The metatarsal gland, identified by its tuft of white hair, is not a predominate scent source.

When a deer travels or stomps its front feet, it leaves scent traces from its interdigital glands. This individual scent is identified by passing deer. Excessive deposits left by a deer stomping its foot will cause alarm when later detected by another deer.

Finally, the pre-orbital and forehead scents are used in marking the branches above primary scrapes along with the buck's saliva. These distinctive combinations appear to be deposited as an attempt at pre-emptive territorial marking. Body language and tail actions of deer can help a hunter anticipate the quarry's intention.

A buck will lay his ears back and lower his antlers, while raising his back and neck hairs, to intimidate another buck into submission. Further, he will approach another buck with a stiff legged, sideways walk to demonstrate his size.

A standing buck, with head held high and lip curled is exhibiting the Flehman posture in an attempt to confirm the presence of an estrous doe by scent detection. While tracking an estrous doe, the buck will travel quickly along her trail, concentrating on the scent with his nose a few inches above the ground and his tail erect in a sexually excited manner. A doe in estrus and ready to breed will hold her tail straight out and slightly to one side, inviting a dominant buck.

Watch closely when deer are standing frozen and alert while using all of their senses to detect any presence of danger. If a doe rotates one ear toward her back trail, she could be listening for the approach of her fawns, or, during the rut period, to the hurried steps of an expectant buck. If she suddenly lays both ears back against her head, she is preparing to flee and is protecting her ears from the slap of brush as she runs.

A slowly rising stiff tail is a sign of alarm or uneasiness and the animal will usually spook from the area immediately. A feeding deer will often flick its tail simultaneously with the raising of its head. A few quick flicks of a lowered tail is more-or-less an all-clear signal and it usually means the deer is contented and preparing to move ahead with normal behavior.

I watched a mature doe one evening on the edge of an alfalfa field as she surveyed the open area. After a thorough review, she extended her tail straight out and wagged it several times like a happy dog. At her signal the lead doe was joined by family and friends for dinner.

An alarmed deer runs with the white underhairs of its flared tail exposed to provide a warning to other deer. A doe instinctively does this so her fawns can easily locate her while they flee from danger. A buck may not raise his tail, which would call attention to him, but instead, might sneak away from danger as covertly as possible.

Be advised that deer may even try to trick the hunter by pretending to relax while they drop their head to feed. Their eyes never leave the suspicious object as they try to induce predator movement. Instantly their head jerks back up, re-inspecting the source of the problem for any change in position or other confirmation of danger. This action is often accompanied by head bobbing as the deer view the subject from slightly different angles, thereby changing the perspective to help identify it.

The age of a deer is of interest to some hunters but the greatest value is for deer herd managers. If considerable younger deer are killed, the herd is healthy and this indicates a status quo or increasing population. If the majority of deer killed are older, this will warn managers of conditions such as a deteriorating habitat or a severe winter with decreased production. The most reliable method for deer aging is by studying their teeth. An article is included in the appendix which thoroughly describes this simple process.

We all know that antlers are not grown for protection from predators since they are dropped early in the winter prior to the most threatening weather conditions when deer are most vulnerable. We also recognize that the number of antler points is not indicative of a buck's age. Rue notes in *The Deer of North America* that most recent research indicates the shape and number of antler points may depend chiefly on heredity, while the size of the antlers is the result of diet.

During a buck's younger years, nutritional intake is mainly directed toward body growth and maturity. After 3 1/2 years, the nutrition can be used to provide greater antler growth, with prime development age from 5 1/2 to 7 1/2 years. Dr. Robert Brown of the Caesar Kleberg Wildlife Research Institute in Kingsville, Texas, determined that bucks take minerals from their own skeletal systems, especially from the ribs and sternum, and deposit them into their antlers. During this period, the ribs become brittle and are easily broken. When antler growth is complete, the minerals are then restored to the temporarily depleted bones.

Antlers have individual shapes like this non-typical buck with extended eye guards. Photo by Ted Rose

Antlers begin growing in April at a rate of about 1/4" per day depending upon nutrition and other factors, and continue until mid-August. This is the fastest form of bone growth known and considerable research is under way on antlers, along with the blood-rich skin covering, called velvet, which is the only regenerating skin membrane among mammals. This phenomenon

This old buckeye buck had multiple beams.

This 177 class, non-typical whitetail, with the unusual double throat patch, was shot by John R. Jeffers, Sr. of antler growth could benefit medical science for cancer victims, burn victims and others. As Kathy Etling reported in her *Outdoor Life* article "Amazing Antlers and How They Grow," several circumstances affect antler shapes. If severe antler damage occurs during growth, the deformed shape of the antler will be repeated the following year and for the rest of the buck's life. Similarly, a broken rear leg will be mirrored by a stunted antler growth on the opposite side, while permanent damage to a front leg will result in a smaller antler on the same side as the foreleg injury. Scientists theorize this antler development compensation by the buck is to lessen the weight on the injured front leg or to help balance the deer as it walks with an injured rear leg, since deer walk by simultaneously raising and lowering opposite front and hind legs.

Several studies involving antler growth have shown interesting results. Even though an occasional doe has grown antlers naturally, scientists have induced antler growth in does with an injection of testosterone. Further studies involve controlling the periods of light, the main criteria stimulating antler growth. This phenomenon called photoperiodicity regulates body responses affecting reproduction, antler growth and other life cycles. Captive mature bucks have grown and shed two sets of antlers in one year by regulating the periods of light they

*Antler growth sequence of 7-year-old "Squirt."
Photographs furnished by Richard English.*

May 6—Growth began mid-April; May 26—Eye guards branch first; June 6—First tine begins to fork

June 30—Unique antler characteristics take shape; August 5—Growth almost complete

were exposed to. By simulating longer and shorter daylight periods, the hormonal release of various glands has altered antler growth times.

On or about the first week in September, antler growth terminates, the velvet dries and is removed. Often the buck wisely eats the shed membrane, which is rich in essential nutrients. Hardening of the antlers, which has already begun, continues throughout the rut and until the antlers are cast, leaving the pedicel which is soon covered by a scab. The new skin under the scab forces it off and will then become the velvet for next year's antlers.

A final note about antlers is intended to dispel some bad teachings that many of us have been exposed to. Thanks to Dr. Kroll's research, we now recognize that a young spike is not necessarily an inferior deer that should be culled before it can breed. As a matter-of-fact, one particularly scraggly specimen, a few years later, emerged from a spike to a trophy 12-point buck with a wide spread.

Knowledge about deer science is a good foundation for hunting strategy. Many successful hunters recognize this and study whitetail facts and tracks to help them determine behavior patterns and increase their hunting pleasure.

Richard English, deer breeder of West Milton, Ohio, with his 320 pound, 7-year-old, 165" class whitetail, "Squirt." Note the antler shape similarities to 6-year-old "Squirt," still in velvet. Photographs furnished by Richard English.

You can fool a deer's eyes most of the time, you can even fool its ears some of the time, but you cannot fool its nose very often.

Bedded buck relies on nose and ears for predator detection. Photo by Rita Ambrose

SURVIVAL BY SENSES

In order for deer to survive nationally and increase from about 500,000 at the turn of the century to near 14 million today, they must be adaptable and have acute senses. Although I truly believe most wild animals, especially deer, have a sixth sense, or telepathic reception to warn them of danger, this chapter deals with their three major protective senses. Deer survive by using their eyes, ears and nose. If a hunter ignores any one of these senses he will probably get the opportunity to hunt all the way back home each trip, with his license still intact. Becoming aware of the limits of each sense will increase your chances of approaching close enough for a clear shot at the vitals.

Since deer are prey animals, they have large bulging eyes, with some areas of binocular vision, and can identify moving predators at long distances. They have good peripheral vision with a viewing arc of about 310°. The remaining 50° creates a blind area directly behind their head. In fact, one morning after a rain, with dripping noises everywhere, a doe passed under my tree. She paused, laid one ear back along her neck, and cocked her head to the side so that she could look rearward. With so much natural noise from the dropping water she could not rely on her ears to detect danger approaching from her blind spot, and had to slightly turn her head to check her backtrail.

If you do not move, it is sometimes possible to fool a deer's eyes. Camouflage clothing helps break a person's silhouette, but remaining absolutely motionless is the most important act of concealment. Do not underestimate the computerlike familiarity that a deer has with its surroundings. Any foreign or new object in their territory will alert them to possible danger. If you are detected but not identified, do not hide from view. If you disappear, the deer will assume you are stalking them and the next time you check, they will be gone. Keeping you in view, the deer will probably circle downwind but may offer an opportunity for a shot before they scent you.

Alerted doe stamps her front foot to warn other deer of potential danger and to startle predator into moving so she can confirm identity.

The ears of a deer twist or rotate individually, allowing them to pick up sounds from two directions simultaneously. The large cupped surfaces help gather and funnel noises for identification. Deer will ignore noises that do not alarm them such as farm tractors or chain saws. I have always wondered if I could walk within shooting range with a running chain saw in one hand and my gun in the other. Even downwind the familiar footfalls of human predators or brush scratching against clothing help deer locate the presence of hunters at long distances. Slow, one or two step walking, with lengthy pauses, along with soft natural clothing fibers such as wool and some cottons will help minimize detection.

Whitetail deer can rotate each ear individually, allowing them to listen in two directions simultaneously.

Their nose is the most sensitive

detection device. As an example: a hound dog can strike a coon trail and after a few steps, trail it in the correct direction. Similarly, a deer can examine a hunter's scent trail that is a few hours old and determine by relative freshness which direction he was headed. When a deer licks its nose, this moistens the surface and allows it to better pick up airborne scents.

When a hunter cleans his body and outer clothing with non-scented soap and bacteria killing shields, and then allows his undergarments to be washed with the family laundry he will smell like a radiant soapsud. In my opinion, a hunter with masking scent smells to a deer like a hunter that has applied skunk or fox urine to his clothing, and not just another friendly woods critter. Get everything you wear clean and if necessary use baking soda as a deodorant. While hunting, dust your body with it, especially areas prone to sweat (hairy parts) such as your groin, underarms, and head.

A deer constantly wets its nose to improve its ability to pick up airborne scents.

Wind is the most important consideration while hunting, especially for bow hunters. When you have a steady breeze, the wind direction is obvious but what about thermals? We all recognize that when the sun rises, convection currents rise and when the sun falls, the wind currents drop. However, beware the early morning thermals just after daylight when the coldest time of the day normally occurs. The thermals during this period are downgrade until the sun raises the air temperatures. Some hunters will use a bic lighter with the fragile flame indicating wind direction or they might tie a thread onto their bow upper limb. I use a small plastic container filled with baking soda. A few squeezes through the uncapped narrow top will spray powder that drifts with the thermal. Whatever method that you use to test wind direction, thermals should be a part of your bowhunting strategy.

Remember, you can fool a deer's eyes most of the time, you can even fool its ears occasionally, but you cannot fool its nose very often.

Hider buck in tall grass is difficult to hunt. Photo by Ted Rose

The distance to long range kills on game is often exaggerated, so too is the distance to misses.

WHITETAIL FALL FEEDING HABITS

Hunters that are consistent understand that the more you know about the habits of your prey, the better your chances of success. They do not leave anything to chance within their control and thereby get more opportunities to sharpen their skinning knives.

The study of animal habits begins with their efforts toward survival. For whitetail deer this would include feeding, breeding, and bedding. For about 50 weeks per year, deer concentrate on feeding, leaving only a couple of weeks to get crazy and breed. While bucks gather in bachelor quarters or live alone, the doe and her family occupy the more generous and accessible bedding sites. These sites are generally in thickets with some food and water included. Deer like to get up during the day, in the seclusion of their bedding area, to stretch, eat a bite or take a drink, and pile up some droppings.

Deer sharing corn, a favorite crop.

Deer are ruminants, meaning an animal with a four chambered stomach. They chew a cud like a cow. Whitetail deer rip food, by action of the lower jaw front teeth pressing against the gum pad on the top of the mouth (no upper front teeth), and quickly swallow while they walk. In this fashion they gather a great deal of food in a short time. When they eat forbs, which means the browse of buds and tender shoots up to the size of a wooden matchstick, they leave a shredded twig end, telltale to the hunter's scouting eye. As you may have observed, deer like to feed into the wind so they can smell danger ahead as they browse, while walking away from any predator trying to stalk from downwind. I have watched deer passing through a freshly cut alfalfa field with grass stringing from their mouths as they chew a few times and then swallow. All foods eaten go into the first, and largest, stomach compartment to be brought up later from the second compartment as partially predigested food and chewed as a cud. Normally, deer like to lie down while cud chewing. That is why you will find beds in the open feeding areas but these are only nighttime feeding beds. They will refill their stomach, which takes 1 to 2 hours, as they retire to the day bed. An adult deer likes to eat 15 to 20 pounds or more of food per day but can go long periods without eating, utilizing its reserves.

Turkey and deer exist together eating many of the same foods.

After a kill, when field dressing is completed, cut open the stomach to see what the deer ate last. It will give you valuable clues to the available food in that area at that time. In the autumn you will soon learn that white oak acorns are whitetails' favorite food, even preferred over red or burr oak. However, in a recent season, the red oak mast in our area was superior to the white and tree stands were located accordingly. An old saying bears attention: "Acorns on the southwest slope will ripen first," due of course to more sunshine. In the middle of October a couple of years ago, strong, gusty winds dropped acorns on the ridges, and the deer sensed it. Later in the season the valley oaks were a better place to hunt. Deer also seem to know instinctively that wind, birds, and squirrels knock down acorns during the day. While they bed, deer get hungry for these nut meats, and from my observations there are about three times more deer at the oak trees in the evening than in the morning. Acorns are high in fats and starches and the deer prefer this food above any other. Hickory nuts are also good, as are beechnuts, although their mast is sporadic. Deer will ignore the walnuts with their hard shells, leaving them for the sharp teeth of the squirrels. A doe will often wean her fawn when the mast drops, and these young deer will never forget the location of the oaks in their area.

Another favorite whitetail attractor food is under the old apple tree. Check there for tracks, droppings, and chewed apples. If many deer visit the orchard, the apples will disappear from the ground, and, in addition, the lower limbs will be picked clean by rearing deer. Following a heavy frost, watch for deer by persimmon trees, and later in the season they will eat the hedgeapple or osage orange fruit.

On the farms, watch the alfalfa and winter wheat fields which provide green food that deer dearly love. Standing corn is another whitetail favorite. With the high cost of storage, farmers often leave their corn in the field through the hunting season providing excellent food and cover for deer. Also, when row crops are harvested, deer will return to glean the fields of spilled corn and soybeans.

In the woods, deer will eat many types of mushrooms which are high in protein and moisture. They will add freshly fallen leaves for roughage especially those from maple and dogwood trees. A main staple is browse of tender shoots, ferns, and other foliage. Look for areas with good understory that deer can easily reach for moisture and nutrition. Forest deer will search out browse areas, especially those sites of recent logging activities or fires.

During the rut, bucks may not eat as much but they do require 3 to 4 quarts of water per day. Therefore, if it is a dry season, a water hole near a doe bedding area could be a great location for a stand. Following the rut, bucks will spend extra time feeding to rebuild their fat reserves prior to winter.

When cold weather arrives, deer will seek spring seeps where ground water keeps temperatures higher, allowing some vegetation to continue growing. Cold weather also keeps deer feeding later in the day since more energy is consumed at these lower temperatures. A few years ago, while hunting in Montana, we spotted deer feeding all day in the -20° temperatures.

If food sources are not concentrated, such as a couple of oak trees in the middle of a maple woods, the trails leading to the major feeding areas would be the best stand locations. When the bedding area is a long distance, as much as one half mile away, it could be after legal shooting hours before deer enter the area and a different strategy must be used. Mature bucks will often hang back in the woods 20-30 yards until nightfall, before coming out into the field to feed. Deer returning to bedding areas from the long distance food source are best hunted in the morning.

Locating the whitetails' favorite fall foods should be a primary goal for the hunter, especially during preseason scouting. This is even more important during the early bow season with the rut at least a month away. Deer will be eating seriously in this season with a final push to add fat for the demands of winter. Find their foods and you will find your deer may sound oversimplified, but it works.

White acorns are a whitetail's favorite food.
Photo by Rita Ambrose

I have noticed that the harder I work at hunting, the luckier I get.

THE PATH OF LEAST RESISTANCE

You should be aware of this instinctive trait of whitetail deer whether scouting, hunting or trailing wounded game. If at all possible, deer will select the path of least resistance.

While scouting, follow trails for convenience, but, be aware of other evidence for future use:
*Look for broken fences or old gates that remain open. A tree that falls across an unused fence and breaks the strands, opens a gate in the woods. Follow old fence rows until you find these deer crossings.

Deer will find sections of broken fence and funnel through the hole.

*Since deer like to bed on ridges that allow them a good view below and a quick release over the crest, look for their bedroom entrance. Check for trails along the most gradual slopes to these high vantage points. They do not like steep slopes either.
*Deer will create a trail along a stream or lake but will not

hesitate to join the water for a quick escape if danger threatens. Scout these trails to headwaters of the lake for the stream crossing. Deer will select a crossing where banks are not too steep and the stream bed is firm, usually at the most shallow portion.
*Notice that the paths wind around brush, rocks, and windfalls. To save energy, deer prefer to duck, or even crawl, under a limb or overhanging briars in lieu of jumping over a downed tree. They prefer to ease along contours on hillsides, rather than crossing them by going up or down a hill.

Deer will walk around obstacles, seeking the easiest route, when they are not under hunting pressure. Photo by Ted Rose

*If you enter a standing cornfield, you will soon confirm that deer take the easiest route between the rows, often just 3 or 4 rows into the planting. Check the fence along the edges of these cultivated fields, keeping in mind that an adult deer stands about 40" high at the shoulder and that a barbed wire fence averages 50" to the top strand. Therefore look for belly hair and mud from hooves on the center strand as deer exit the feeding area, ducking under the top strand, instead of jumping over.

Deer hunters must always expect the unexpected but should hunt with the odds for consistency:
*Most hunters know that a deer prefers to move through the woods easily and silently with the least resistance possible. For that reason, trail watching is both popular and productive. In the past I have been fooled by deer that veered off their trail to funnel down my cleared shooting lane toward my ground blind while looking directly at me and not allowing enough movement to prepare for a shot.

... and they actually use it!

*It is important to recognize that deer prefer flat areas for bedding, breeding or trails. You will find their beds and locate scrapes in these level sites. Because of that, the flat top of a ridge, a valley bottom, or a bench along a side slope is the best area to focus your hunting efforts.
*To eliminate noise, deer will circle loose stone zones.
*All game likes to walk in intermittent stream beds where runoff water has washed out leaves and other debris.
*A deer that has been shot at will often head for an opening, even into a field, to facilitate a quick escape with no restrictions.
    Wounded animals are more difficult to pattern or generalize. Depending on the severity of the wound, hunting pressure, and other factors, they may panic, and not use all of their instinct to seek the easiest route to survival:
*A wounded deer seeking to escape will typically backtrack along the route that it used to enter the area. From recent passage, it knows that it is safe.

This button buck is just one of the half million deer killed annually on our nation's highways.

*A mortally wounded deer will retreat based mainly on terrain, as quickly, and with as little effort as possible, often following a downhill route using less energy.

If you look for the path of least resistance, you will be a better hunter, since you will be reacting to the instinctive behavior of the whitetail deer.

Fawns enjoying a snack

The three most important factors when bow hunting are: wind, wind and wind.

LET THE WEATHER HELP CUT THE NOTCHES IN YOUR DEER LICENSE

You cannot shoot your deer while you are sitting at home in your easy chair. That reminds me of the time that I elk hunted near Cripple Creek, Colorado and the owner of the inn reported that most of the elk around there were killed on Mahogany Ridge. That night I searched the local maps in vain for that particular area. The next evening, after the day's hunt, I again asked where they had been seeing elk, with the same response, "most of the elk were killed on Mahogany Ridge." When I pulled out my map and asked for directions, he just laughed and pointed to the bar . . . with the mahogany wood top.

Inclement weather can be tough hunting, but deer hunters with knowledge of the hunting area and the proper equipment can make it work for their benefit.

Snow allows a hunter to see deer much better while following tracks to locate where they have been. Keep in mind that deer can also see farther away, especially when the hunter is moving. A dry snow can help cover stalking noises but a stand is still usually the best way to hunt unless you have adequate hunters for a drive.

Deer have good insulation and a high threshold of pain and are not affected by low temperature in terms of discomfort. However, they instinctively know that more of their stored energy is used during these cold periods and they may stay bedded longer, arising to feed only during the warmest part of the day to conserve energy. Forest deer, with limited food supplies, will feed longer in cold weather or on days following moonless nights. Look for them to bed in thermal growths such as pine groves, dense thickets, swamps with cattails, or even thick stands of broom grass.

In a fog or heavy mist, deer move with confidence as

The cover of snow can allow a hunter to approach close enough for a shot. Photo by John Maxwell

though it were nighttime. If you know of an active low-land runway along a creek, it would be a good time for a stand nearby. Often these conditions include damp ground to help decrease boot noise and stillhunting can be attempted. Keep in mind if you hunt with a scope that it will magnify the moisture in the atmosphere and actually be worse than open sights. On overcast days, without normal daylight intensity, deer tend to feed later and then hurry along trails to the bedding area with less caution.

If the weather is a steady light rain, deer will ignore it, with business as usual. Get some good raingear and keep hunting. If there is a slight breeze on these rainy days at least the wind direction is predictable and this provides the best conditions for stillhunting. Mature deer will select a bedding site that will allow the prevailing wind to bring them scents of danger from behind, while they watch in front for approaching hunters.

A storm changes everything. Rain, with relentless high winds, especially a gusting wind, will excite and scare the nervous whitetail. They will detect odors one second and nothing the next, with changes occurring too quickly to identify or pinpoint the source. There is noise everywhere and continuous movement which results in blocked senses and confusion. The deer know that they are at a disadvantage in the storm and lie low. They will leave the big woods for dense cover. They prefer a thicket of short, durable trees like pinoak, thornapple or a young pine planting. To protect themselves from the wind they will seek cover on the lee slopes. During a swirling wind storm, deer will primarily use their eyes to detect danger and oftentimes the stillhunter in this situation will find himself/herself eye to eye with a bedded deer. Bowhunting under these conditions is extremely difficult. If a major storm occurs at night, deer will be feeding the next day, especially if it was a 10 or 12 hour storm. When the storm ends, regardless of the time of day, deer will be up and feeding. Small openings in dense cover near bedding areas will generally produce animals. If a storm is extremely severe and long lasting, deer have been known to bed for several days. Animals can sense a quickly falling barometer and will feed before the storm arrives. Therefore, the best times to stand hunt would be immediately before and right after a major storm.

Hunters can get into a rut too. For example: on dry, still days, there is no need to attempt stillhunting, and on a windy day as a front comes through, do not waste your time in a stand. The best hunting will occur when you concentrate on conditioning your mind, body, and spirit into a positive attitude. Whatever the weather you will then become a better woodsman and a more successful hunter.

Always keep in mind that we each have the capability to accidently shoot another person while we are hunting.

DRIVE FOR KNOWLEDGE

The question is; "Should youngsters learning to hunt whitetail deer be used as drivers?" Is this a safe and productive method which could be followed to teach new hunters about deer?

During the early 1950's there were no tree stands or hot seats in our deer camps. Hunting was a social interaction and driving was the only accepted method of hunting in the small midwestern town where I grew up. You were either a driver or you took your turn on a stand. The stand, which meant just that, not a sit, was usually located at the base of a large tree and used year after year. Shotguns, almost exclusively 12 gauge, with rifled slugs or pumpkin balls (round lead balls the size of a dime) using the standard bead shotgun front sight were the sportsmans' choice. The ability to hit a target the size of a stop sign at 60 yards was indeed a bragging feat. With only a few days each year to hunt, just seeing a whitetail deer would often constitute an entire hunting season. If you actually got a deer, the entire county referred to you, as "a deer hunter."

Hunting camp—the early years.

During that period, as a teenager, I did not own a legal deer gun so I hunted without a gun. Through the friendship of two adults, I was allowed to join the men in their deer drives. However, most of the men in the group did not want the responsibility of watching out for a youngster.

Of course with no gun, I automatically became one of the drivers. In many ways this served to be a very valuable deer hunting apprenticeship. Usually I saw more deer than any of the other hunters while learning about deer trails and traits. At first, I would excitedly ask the standers if they had also seen the two does or the monster buck (any deer with antlers) and generally received a negative sarcastic response. The thought of a thirteen year old kid, without even a gun, seeing a deer was in itself ludicrous. After a few disbelieving ridicules, I kept silent on the sightings, and after 40 years of hunting, this habit has stayed with me.

Since it seemed inconsistent to make noises while sneaking through the woods, I was a silent driver. In addition, I inadvertently traveled through the woods with the trick of an experienced hunter. For balance, to poke puff balls, to dislodge spider webs or maybe for my own security, I always broke a branch to use as a cane while driving. Unknowingly, this third leg disrupted the cadence of a two legged predator and helped me approach to within close range of several deer without alarming them. My hearing was good in those days but my sight has always been my keenest sense. As in mushroom hunting, you see more details when you are stopped. Therefore, without realizing it, I was stillhunting as I slowly hurried through the thickets and woods patches toward the waiting standers, stopping often to inspect the area ahead. During rabbit season, while hunting with my .22 single shot rifle, I would often spot the rabbit's eye and shoot them sitting. It never occurred to me that a large elusive animal, like a whitetail deer, would sit tight while being hunted. Therefore, I expected to see the whole deer or nothing at all. Later, I learned to look ahead for deer parts such as a leg, antler, black nose or patch of white hair. An unforgettable experience came on one drive through a deciduous woods when I dropped into a flat, low land near a small creek. After walking past an area of cattails and bunch grass, the size of my living room, I heard a frantic scurrying behind me. I looked over my shoulder in time to see a white flag behind a broad set of antlers disappear down my back trail. This is the first time that I have admitted this to anyone. On that day I felt ashamed, since I had failed to drive the buck ahead of me to the expectant standers. The image of this fleeing mature buck and the bed that I examined in the small area of ground cover are still etched in my memory.

Alert deer with tail hairs flared are a typical sight for a driver. Photo by Ted Rose

Occasionally I observed deer circling back between other drivers and one time saw a buck disappear in a field of knee high weeds. While I watched the empty field, he reappeared momentarily along the edge as he gathered to jump the border fence and bound into the nearby woods.

In those days hunter orange was not yet a color. It would have sounded more like a cold drink after a hot day in the field to us. Safety was not as important as getting a shot at a deer. My black knit hat pulled over my head rode above a ragged old wool gray and black plaid coat. Although this hunter color code most resembled a whitetail deer, it was very typical outerwear in those days.

It would surprise me how often I would locate a stander by seeing him silhouetted against the snow or some other open background. Sometimes I would catch sight of that telltale upward arm movement as he wiped his nose while having no idea that I had driven to within 50 yards directly in front of him. I remember that I would fight the temptation to see how close I could approach without being detected or maybe even to slip past unnoticed. To alert them to my presence, I would whistle like a bobwhite. If this failed to get his attention, I would wave both arms above my head until spotted, wondering why it took so long to get the standing adult to identify me even though I could clearly see his face.

Sure, I was a driver for the benefit of the adults, but at the same time I was studying and learning basic deer habits. I knew the location of virtually every bedding area for both bucks and does. I located their escape routes and found which trails were active during hunting season. I watched as the deer maneuvered around all of us. It certainly gave me more respect for the evasive tactics possessed by a mature whitetail deer. After bumping a deer, especially if I could identify it by sex and size, I would take time to study the track size, placement and distance between tracks at various speeds. Once I watched a buck easily jump all the way across a lane cut through the woods. It was as though he knew that the lane hunter would not see his tracks and therefore never know that he existed.

Now, when someone asks me to take his youngster hunting, I wonder if it would be acceptable to clothe him in hunter orange and make him drive to hunt. Somehow this seems dangerous or wrong to make the novice a driver. The possibility of him getting lost or injured worries me, so I usually place him on a stand along an escape route and drive toward him myself, even though I realize that being a stand hunter can be a tough, cold, boring way to learn about deer and deer hunting. It may be that in everyone's best interest, I should make young hunters slowly walk the woods placing myself on stand to intercept them or any deer that they drive toward me. Can you imagine the reputation society would award to me if I would teach youngsters how to hunt by making personal driving dogs out of them? Fortunately, you can probably justify this action for your own children or those of a close relative while teaching them about deer.

For my own part, I sure appreciate the whitetail knowledge that I gained during those early years while driving for the adults of my hometown.

The only thing worse than stillhunting in the rain is stillhunting when the woods are bone dry.

*Stillhunt extremely slowly and you may get a shot before an alerted deer identifies you and escapes.
Photo by Ted Rose*

HOW DO I HUNT THEE? LET ME COUNT THE WAYS

Whether you stand, sit, walk, crawl or float, if you are out there hunting, at least you have a chance to bag a deer. Stand hunting may be the most popular and also the most productive for whitetail deer but other methods can be effective as well as exciting. Stillhunting requires certain skills and conditions while drive hunting needs two or more hunters. Floating in a canoe can be a great adventure if you have access to the proper waterways. Generally speaking, when deer are moving, your best technique is to stand, but when deer are not moving, you must walk.

Stands can be either in a tree or on ground level. The old stump sitters recognized the need to be comfortable on stand to maintain the disciplines of patience and motionless watching. Remaining on stand patiently waiting for a prescouted deer to arrive requires confidence in your ability to correctly predict deer activity. Keep in mind that after opening day of firearms season, a deer's routine may be greatly changed. Knowledge of local deer activity allows you to stand where whitetails are usually seen.

Probably the most appropriate axiom of stand hunting is: Arrive early, stay late, and bring your lunch. In other words, hunt all day. This is especially true at times when deer are moving naturally such as during the frenzied activity of the rut period. It can also be productive on stand when other hunters are in the woods. Clumsy stillhunters are the stand hunters friends and this is a good time to be on stand along an escape route or in dense cover.

If you intend to remain in a stand for long periods, avoid drinking caffeinated beverages like regular coffee, tea or colas. They are diuretics causing you to urinate frequently. Drink water, decaffeinated beverages or soup for moisture.

Stand hunters must always be alert, expecting to see a deer at any moment. Concentrate your attention on heavy cover near travel routes for sneaking deer. Although I consider myself an extremely alert hunter, I hate to admit how many times I have caught a glimpse of nearby motion and glanced in that direction expecting to see a bird or squirrel but was surprised to see one or more deer. They seemed to materialize from nowhere and would be below my stand with no warning. Utilize the deer near your stand to indicate the presence of other deer. For example: A deer passing below on the trail that keeps looking toward its back trail, without alarm, is likely being followed by other deer, frequently a buck.

During extremely cold or windy hunting conditions, it is warmer, safer and steadier on the ground. If the area that you hunt is hilly terrain, the selection of an elevated stand could be a ground blind. This is one of the bowhunters best kept secrets. A ground stand in a natural blind such as a downed tree top can be very effective. A wise hunter, especially on an evening hunt, must take all precautions when entering his stand. Approach your stand with as much concealment, as little noise and as minor a scent contamination as possible. On at least three occasions, I have watched deer as they observed a hunter walk along a field edge into his evening stand. The alerted deer then went a different direction.

If you are going to stillhunt, learn the area thoroughly. Locate trails and bedding areas while shed hunting or scouting. Deer have a decided home-court advantage, not to mention their acute senses. A hunter that just walks into an unknown woods usually has about as much chance of success as a person playing Bingo, and searching for B-5 in the G column. The trick to stillhunting is to see unalarmed whitetail deer and be in a position where you are concealed from identification. This hunting method at least gives you a chance at a shot by stalking the deer instead of just hoping that they will pass by your stand. You will soon discover that stillhunting is more mental than physical so that an occasional stump sit is necessary to allow you to relax and regain your full concentration before continuing on foot. The young, strong hunter's premise is: The more ground that I cover, and the harder I hunt, the better my chance of success. What we have here is the young bull-old bull folly. Covering long distances is not a practical goal for stillhunters.

Some ground conditions are just not suitable for stillhunting. With a frost, crusted snow or dry leaves, it is almost impossible to approach close to deer without being heard. Not only is a soft, damp ground beneficial, but the hunter's footwear is also critical. For quiet moving, a soft, flexible sole that allows you to feel every stick and stone through it is necessary. By rolling your foot, heel to toe, you imitate a four footed animal's double step sound. Take only one or two steps at a time, and then carefully inspect every detail ahead. Focus on a white spot that may be the patch of hair on the throat of a deer or a black spot that could turn out to be a deer's nose. Look for a horizontal shape which could be the back of a deer. Check the slightest motion in case it might reveal a rotating deer ear. Learn to look for parts of a deer as opposed to an entire deer. If you accidentally snap a branch, wait for several minutes before continuing and the deer will likely forget the noise location. Wool or brushed cotton clothes that eliminate scratching noises should be worn. Carry a pair of bypass blade hand pruners (not the anvil type blade), so that you can quietly remove a branch, briar or vine from across your path. Use the deer trails and shuffle along with noises similar to deer passing. Some hunters will remove their boots or pull a sock over them to soften their footstep for a final stalk. Your speed should be s l o w e r t h a n s l o w, while you use your binoculars to penetrate the area ahead and on both sides. When you spot a deer, study it to determine its activity, whether it is alone and its destination if moving. While stillhunting in pines or other thick cover, kneel or squat down to look under lower branches. This is a good opportunity to use your binocs to spot deer legs or even a bedded deer. Whitetails try to bed where they will not be disturbed by hunters, so hunt where no one else goes. They will hide in small areas of cover where it is safe, but also where areas of escape cover are not too far away in case they are detected. If you are looking into a small patch of dense cover, and have eye contact with a hider, they will spook instantly.

Stillhunting in soft snow allows hunter to approach closely to feeding animals. Photo by John Maxwell

During the day, when a storm is ending, it is a good time to hunt dense thickets and known bedding areas to catch deer in their bed or up feeding. Stop adjacent to trees that help break up your silhouette but do not lean on small trees that will shake the leaves and reveal your location. If you bump a deer from its bed, it may circle back, especially if it has not scented or identified you. Most whitetails spooked in heavy cover will run only a hundred yards or so before settling down and you may still be able to stalk into shooting position. Every season I have several opportunities for a stalk, either on feeding or bedded deer.

Since cornfields are a natural deer magnet, providing food and cover, you should attempt to hunt there. If alone, and you have a breezy day, stillhunting these unharvested fields is a possibility from downwind. Admittedly, it is very difficult to draw your bow and maintain a steady shooting posture as you carefully lean through the corn row for a shot. I have stalked to within 20 yards of several bedded deer in standing corn while bowhunting but have yet to be on target accurately enough to release an arrow. By firearms season, the corn harvest is usually complete.

Cornfields can better be driven when your group gets together. Safety should be the highest priority in any drive. Blaze orange hats and jackets should be worn by all of the hunters. If possible, drive with the wind while the standers take positions downwind.

If your group organizes a drive, one person, familiar with the terrain, escape routes and local deer habits, must be in charge. The standers should go to the exact location assigned and stay until the drive is completed. A common mistake is to locate too close to the security area so the standers are detected by the deer before the drive begins and they sneak between hunters. The standers should move into their position where the undisturbed deer do not see, hear or smell them. Every stander should conceal themselves where they have a clear view of their shooting zone. This individual zone is the only direction that a stander can shoot without jeopardizing the drivers or another stander. All standers should be ready prior to the beginning of the drive since wary deer, especially those familiar with drive tactics, will dislodge and escape if they even suspect that a drive is being organized. Standers owe it to the drivers and other standers to be very alert. Even veteran hunters acknowledge that deer will suddenly appear 20 to 30 yards from the nearest cover. They had walked to this point without being spotted so you can imagine how many deer sneak past without even being detected. Drivers should move slowly and silently, letting their scent drift ahead of them to move deer without spooking them into a running escape. If you are attempting to drive a thicket by yourself with your partner on stand, use a zig-zag pattern, changing direction often, as you slowly penetrate the dense areas.

After opening day in Michigan, our camp drives the potholes, which are small depressions grown up with saplings around small ponds or swamps. Standers surround the potholes while the remaining hunters tromp through the low areas spooking deer to hunters waiting on the ridges. Special care must be exercised in this fast paced hunt not to shoot toward another hunter.

Suitable waterways, where hunting is permitted, lend themselves to some of the best deer hunting available. Be sure to check the float hunting regulations in your state. On a lake float hunt during muzzleloader season, I happened to glance over my shoulder and spot a buck running across the dam. Knowing that a path led around the deep end and joined a trail that led to a honeysuckle thicket, I paddled furiously to the far bank, jumped out and ran about 300 yards to a position that overlooked this trail. Sure enough, in about the time it took me to catch my breath, along came the buck sneaking as fast as he safely could. My percussion cap failed to fire as the dark haired ten-point momentarily paused on the trail not more than 25 yards away. Even though I did not get the buck, I had satisfactorily predicted his route and was able to intercept him by canoeing across the lake.

A canoe allows the hunter to make a silent approach into dense border areas alongside water where humans are expected by the deer to arrive on foot with telltale noises. This works well on streams as well as lakes. A popular strategy is to drop one hunter above thick river bottom cover while the other hunter quietly floats downstream and takes a stand along the bank. The first hunter then stillhunts toward the waiting hunter creating a short drive through the thick cover. Hunters can spend the entire day leapfrogging their way downstream in this manner. With a small boat or canoe, it also makes transporting deer out of the woods a lot easier.

The most effective type of hunting method(s) on a specific day will depend on the number of hunters in camp, the weather and the terrain. Varying conditions will dictate the preferred method and the best equipment to be used. Deer do not always cooperate by behaving predictably but one fact always remains true. . . . You will never put a sag in the meat pole while sitting on your donkey in camp.

The Nobel family float hunting.

*As hunting season approaches,
it is time to soften up your boots
and harden up your muscles.*

ON THE TRAIL

Scouting season runs from January 1 to December 31 inclusive, with a little time off for hunting. Scouters should be: not seen, not heard and not smelled. This is especially true while scouting just prior to or during hunting season. To keep from alarming deer, travel scent free, or wear a cover scent while scouting in sensitive areas.

Scout in late summer to verify trophy bucks. Photo by Ted Rose

Preseason scouting is mainly to locate the current food source. Scouting during hunting season is to verify food source and possibly to look for active primary scrapes. Post season scouting is to locate active trails, escape routes, bedding areas and to review stand sites. Early spring scouting is to check deer activity and to hunt for sheds. Midsummer field activity is scheduled to perform minor trimming on existing stand sites while selecting and clearing new ones. Late summer scouting is to observe deer activity while estimating maturity and score of bucks.

Since you should already be familiar with the main bedding areas, you simply need to confirm the food source for the deer a few days ahead of the season opener. Scout with binocs or a spotting scope to confirm deer time schedules. Eliminate as much human scent contamination as possible. These odors will do more to disturb a deer's routine that anything else.

If you see a buck during scouting that you plan to hunt, check his tracks for any peculiarities that might help identify him, such as a nick on the hoof or one side shorter than the other. This will let you know, when you check tracks during the season, of your deer's travel routes or where-a-bouts.

Patience is extremely important to be a consistently successful scouter. It allows you to intently concentrate on detail, perceive every woods sign and detect presence of all game. It goes beyond your three detection senses and helps make you a woods wise scouter. While some scouters have this ability instinctively, woods patience can be developed with practice. A positive mental attitude is essential for a productive scout.

While late summer scouting for bucks, you will notice that sightings become less frequent in September as they become more nocturnal. The bucks, especially the younger ones, are in their bachelor groups during this time. While older bucks will sometimes hang out together, they often prefer to remain as loners. Whitetail deer in the upper half of the United States and in Canada will normally shed their velvet during the first week of September and you should look for saplings, brush or grapevines where these rubs have occurred.

Prior to the season, when other hunters are just beginning to think about the hunt, spend time in the field patterning deer. Trail timers with trip clocks are nice, but a poor man's trail monitor will work fine. Simply stretch a fine thread across the deer trail at shoulder height. It can indicate the passage of a buck and the direction that he was going. Of course, it could be another scouter, so put it where tracks are visible and you can confirm your deer. Several threads, checked regularly, can help pattern a buck's travel route. Natures trail monitors can also provide information. Eating spider webs is not pleasant but at least you are assured that another scout or hunter has not preceded you on the trail. Low webs, still intact, indicate that no deer have used that trail for a while either.

Take a compass while scouting to check wind direction on different days. This will confirm prevailing wind and also determine varying wind directions caused by rivers, valleys, hills or other geographic features.

Spotlighting is a sensitive issue to-the general public and other hunters. With no gun or bow of any kind in your vehicle, it is legal in some states to use a light to locate deer. If you intend to scout this way, I suggest that you advise your local sheriff or game department official of the time and location of your activity. Be aware that rural residents and landowners may have had some bad experiences with poachers jacklighting in the area and hostile confrontations could occur.

During the season you might scout for active primary scrapes or rub lines to hunt near. Some scrapes are active past hunting season, well into the winter, and these popular sites, possibly licking branches, should be recorded and regarded as a good location to hunt next season. If you find soft, moist, shiny deer droppings during scouting, they are fresh,

A few days old snow, after the season, will help you locate trails of undisturbed deer.

perhaps only a few hours old, while hard, fibrous, dry ones are older.

Scout directly after the hunting season ends since the deer's reaction will be indicative of heavy hunting pressure and therefore escape routes can be more easily located.

While selecting your stand site, kneel down occasionally so you can get a view from the same perspective as that of an adult deer. While checking a ridge top treestand one winter, I discovered why a buck had spooked from the trail during hunting season. From a kneeling position on the deer trail, I found that my stand was silhouetted by an opening in the tree limbs behind it.

When you scout for your best stand site, do not forget to scout for your best access trail to this special stand. Pick a route that will avoid feeding areas, does not cross the main trail, remains downwind and can be followed in the dark.

One of the main scouting goals is to locate bedding areas. Beds that you discover in open field edges, orchards or harvested crop fields are likely nighttime resting beds. Whitetails do not spend all night feeding, but gather for a few hours and then bed to chew their cud and rest. Security beds are strategically located areas that deer return to during the day. They are selected because they offer protection from predators. Most bedding areas provide cover, advantageous ground conditions (cool in summer,

Deer scrape snow out of bed and locate where they will have a good view of the surrounding terrain.

warm in winter), some food, good wind detection, a vantage point and emergency escape routes. Single beds in thick cover will usually indicate a mature buck.

Backtrack from feeding areas while scouting in snow to locate bedding sites. During the first week in January, I backtracked from a harvested corn field to find an area with over 16 beds. This particular herd contained five animals, so I knew that they had been frequenting the same bedding area.

Look for stream crossings. This is a primary location for funneled activity in the deer woods. Deer prefer a firm bottom, in a shallow part of the stream with gradual banks for easiest crossing sites.

You can observe terrain much better with the leaves off of the trees and a snow cover. This is one of the best times to get out and simply follow trails. It may allow you to find the minor side trails that parallel the main trails. These faint paths are often preferred by mature bucks.

When spring finally arrives, spend time in the woods hunting for shed antlers. The dropped antlers that you find in March or April confirm that the buck survived hunting season and the winter. The location where you find these sheds is probably a place where the buck feels safe and frequents.

After determining the area where you plan to hunt and obtaining permission from the landowner, the next most important step is the location of your stand(s). Scouting is necessary to pattern deer movement and to pinpoint the most advantageous stand site. The use of quad or aerial maps may give you some guidance as to the most logical places to look, but field reconnaissance will be required to confirm deer travel routes and select specific stand trees or ground blind sites.

Obtain a quad map which has a scale of 1"=2000 feet and then have your 80 acres, or whatever size your hunting area is, enlarged several times. This will give you space to record trails, rubs, primary scrapes, bedding areas, food sources, etc. If the area is agricultural, copies can be updated each year, with crops rotated to help analyze the most productive deer trails.

Just obtaining permission to hunt on private land is becoming more difficult. If possible, use a mutual friend as a reference when you approach a landowner. Wear casual clothes and visit them in your pickup truck. Most people will be more likely to let a friend hunt on their land, so try to make friends first and permission to hunt may be granted to you later. If unfamiliar with local landowners, approach the farmer during July or one of his least busy months. Never attempt to gain hunting permission during planting or harvest season when the owner's time is limited and his attention is elsewhere. On your first visit, take your wife with you, instead of a bunch of other hunters, so the landowner can see that you are a family person.

List your participation with hunting clubs and organizations and describe your activities that promote safe and ethical hunting so that he can see you are conscientious and serious about your sport. Give him a reason to trust you so that he will be comfortable allowing you to enter his property.

In addition to carrying binocs every time you enter the field, take a note pad and pencil to record information. Write down sightings, possible stand sites, or other pertinent data. For a sighting, record date, time of day, number and sex of deer, undisturbed location and direction of travel, escape route if alarmed, wind direction, weather conditions and what the deer were feeding on. Other data might include location where sheds were found, rubs, scrapes, estimated antler score of mature bucks, etc. If you maintain a journal of data, a schedule of deer activities and their habits will be easier to analyze and probably more reliable.

If you plan to hunt standing cornfields, preliminary scouting can help to narrow down the probable bedding sites. During planting, locate the areas of ground within the field that are slightly higher. Check the field again after vegetation spraying and cultivation, when corn is knee high. If there are weeds growing in the areas where there is also a slight rise in the ground, locate these spots by referencing them to trees or posts at the field edge both ways. Deer like to bed on slightly elevated ground, especially if weeds are growing between the rows. When the wind is right, hunt toward these pre-selected spots.

Scout year round to learn as much as possible about your deer area and your hunting time will be more efficient and rewarding. Practice woods patience so that you learn to concentrate better and you will not only become a veteran sign reader but this habit will carry over to improve your hunting skills.

Deer like to bed in tall grass.

Everyone is a trophy hunter on opening day.

O.D. SUCCESS

In many states, especially those with a short firearms season, opening day (O.D.) is the one day, by far, when the greatest number of whitetail kills are reported. Not only are more hunters in the field that day, but undisturbed deer are less cautious which helps make O.D. special. There are two distinctive opening days. Bow hunters do not impact the deer routine like firearm nimrods do, so the gun O.D. is more critical. Further, the O.D. of firearms season in heavily hunted areas provides two separate strategies for the learned hunter. The first technique involves the deers' routine from sunrise shooting hours until about 10 AM. The second strategy will start some time after 10 AM and last throughout the day. Since the deer are usually bedded by midmorning, a variation in hunting tactics would be typical for most stand locations by that time. If your early morning stand location is based on a result of scouting the deer travel routes between the feeding and bedding area, you should be successful unless another hunter has intercepted the deer closer to the feeding area. Open feeding areas might be good locations on O.D. morning if they involve fields off of the main road and out of sight of homes. If the rut period is peaking, you might be better advised to concentrate on this breeding activity when locating your stand.

An alternate to stand relocation during mid-morning would be to initially occupy a position along an escape route or in a thick security zone such as a swamp. A funnel of woodland, where the forest narrows, is a good choice, adjacent to a heavily hunted area. This might be slow hunting early on, but the possibilities would increase with increased activity of other hunters. It will not take very long for an experienced deer, that has survived at least one season, to figure out that the season has opened.

The one effort that will maximize your success is to hunt all day. Mental conditioning relates to the desire and drive of the individual. Physical preparedness means getting your body into condition, but equally important, you must follow the proper diet for strength and endurance.

Correct foods will not totally compensate for poor physical conditioning but a proper diet will provide you with adequate nutritional requirements for most hunting situations. Obviously, stand hunters do not exert as much energy as mountain climbing hunters but they still have to haul their deer out.

What you eat the day before O.D. will determine your energy levels for that special event. This period before the hunt is when your body should be given the opportunity to store up all the complex carbohydrates that it can. Foods containing starches including pasta, cereals, whole wheat bread, fruit, grains and certain vegetables are excellent sources. Balance your meal with foods containing simple carbohydrates such as soft drinks, pastries, candy and more fruit.

Protein, such as meat, takes longer to digest and is not a good pre-opener food. Also, stay away from spicy foods or ones that promote gas production.

Liquid intake is more important than most of us realize. Adequate amounts of water can actually provide greater endurance. It also prevents dehydration which is a major cause of altitude sickness or headaches.

Snacks during the day while hunting are necessary to maintain energy levels. Some foods are not easily digested and converted into energy and therefore do not make a good trail snack. Nuts, cheese and smoked meats are examples of this slow digesting category. A snack is intended to provide the hunter with quick energy which is supplied from simple carbohydrates. Fruits are the best source since candy bars might create an immediate surge followed by a lowering energy level. Other good items for a trail snack would be dried fruit, granola bars or oatmeal/raisin cookies. My favorite trail mix is simply equal amounts of raisins and chocolate chips mixed together. I also carry a pouch of homemade venison jerky which seems to adequately satisfy my hunger while hunting all day. Make sure that you do not wrap your snacks in noisy paper which rattles every time you reach for a mouthful.

Some people claim that fanatic hunters will try almost anything which improves their chances for deer. It must be true because for several seasons I ate two alfalfa pills a day during the month before, and for the entire length of the bow season. I was convinced that my human odor from perspiration and breath would be less offensive and less detectable by deer.

O.D. hunts are not always a success but they usually provide at least an opportunity for the persistent hunter. October 11 was the O.D. for bow season, but the morning hunt was unsuc-

Hunting during the noon hour paid off when this 11-point moved through heavy cover.

cessful. I watched the deer meander off of their normal trail to browse their way into the bedding area too far away for a shot. It had been a dry fall and stillhunting on this quiet day would be too difficult so I stayed out of the bedding areas. Mid-day was spent quietly scouting areas to see what feeding or breeding activity was under way. The white acorn mast had started to fall and the squirrels in the oak trees convinced me that all the animals were aware of this desirable food source. At 2:30 PM, I moved my portable stand into the oak woods and set up. It was 5 PM before the shadow of a young 6-point joined me. As he approached one of my previously cut shooting windows, noisily shelling acorns with his mouth, I came to full draw. Before offering a clear shot, he changed direction, turned his back to me, and retraced his steps searching the ground for acorns that he had missed. With my aching arms now shaking, I had to make a decision. Occasionally, when letting off my draw, using the mechanical release, my arrow had un-nocked and fallen to the ground. I could not chance this error with the buck so close. Picking a small opening between the branches, I sighted on a clear spot 30 yards past the deer and shot. The buck jumped as the arrow struck the ground but continued eating when he could see no danger there. Finally, he returned to my shooting lane and I released another arrow, which appeared to be a perfect shot through his vitals.

What happened next made me a dedicated oak woods hunter. Within a few minutes of the 6-point running off, two doe entered the small cluster of oak trees to feed. Since I had purchased both of my archery tags prior to the season, I nocked another arrow. When one of the does passed below my stand, my bow season was over, but the work had just begun. I could not find the arrow used on the 6-point and since his trail was spotty and difficult to follow, I returned to the doe. With the help of a friend we found her in a few minutes of trailing. Darkness and a sudden rain storm kept us from following the buck until morning light, even though we tried to trail using our flashlights. The blood spots were 10 to 50 feet apart and to add to the confusion, the heavily bleeding doe had joined the bucks escape route, causing us to loose his trail. Finally, late the next morning, we stumbled across the 6-point who had left almost no blood trail in his one quarter mile run. The arrow had passed almost exactly through the center of his body as the errant shot was too far back and had cut through the diaphragm without hitting a vital organ. Only the honed sharpness of the blade, with internal bleeding, had killed the buck. The thick damp foliage of the creek bottom kept the deer cool until we found him and fortunately all of the meat was saved.

On November 11, the same year, it was firearms O.D. and I was hunting with my 50 caliber muzzleloader. It was a frosty

Author with O.D. 6-point.

morning and the rut was active, so I selected a ground stand along a trail near a bedding area where an active scrape was located. Around the scrape and in the trail, under cover of darkness, I applied doe-in-heat to some weeds. I then took a position sitting at the base of a tree downwind with my back to the bedding thicket. At 7:15 AM, a non-typical 8-point caught the scent of the lure as he was entering the thicket. He surprised me as I spotted him sneaking from behind, about 40 yards to my right. He was too close to allow me to raise my gun in the stillness of the morning. After checking the scrape, he continued on the scent trail, circling right back to my shooting lane, frequently dropping his nose to the ground before looking eagerly ahead for the doe. Each time he dropped his head to verify the hot doe scent, I quietly maneuvered further into shooting position. At a distance of about 30 yards, the buck suddenly became aware of my existence. Frozen on the trail, his neck stretching high for a positive identification, his tail raised in alarm, he knew it was too late. The muzzle of my caplock was waiting at that opening in the trail and my sights were already fixed on his lungs. He did not run far. Although his hocks were darkened with recent use, his neck was not too swollen. Curiously, when skinned, I found that the deformed left antler was the result of a skull fracture that had not completely healed. Light hunting pressure during the bow season had not disturbed his routine nor forced him into becoming a nocturnal feeder.

After O.D., the routines of deer may change but they still

use their favorite bedding areas. This may be a good stand location if you can enter the bedding area without disturbing deer in their feeding areas and are settled into your stand long before daylight. Deer under heavy hunting pressure, that feed nocturnally, will get hungry and browse on forbs during the day in the security of their bedding areas. This may afford the patient hunter additional opportunities for a shot.

Never ignore the intensity of the rut, whatever the hunting pressure in an area. Also keep in mind that whitetail deer pattern hunters, and noisy activity at camp means that the woods are again safe for the wary deer to move. Many experienced hunters who prepare themselves by eating the proper foods, hunt the noon time hours, and are rewarded for their efforts with O.D. bucks.

Non-typical 8-point made opening day successful.

Every time that a shot breaks the stillness, it is an abrupt reminder that other hunters share the woods.

BREAKING THE SILENCE

After practicing all of your hunting life to make a noise like a bushel of apples, it is awkward to break the silence of the woods. Whether you use a pair of antlers in a rattling session, or you thrash a sapling with a single antler, it takes away the hunter's element of surprise. Now the deer know that something is there, they have pinpointed the location, and, if all works well, they will come hunting for you. Do not underestimate the accuracy in which the whitetail deer has located the rattling source. They will readily walk right under your tree. This creates a condition in which you must remain absolutely motionless if you expect to succeed, since the deer will use his eyes more than usual looking for the bucks that he has recently heard.

The best antlers to use for your rattling set should come from a recently killed buck (even a road kill). Old antlers or bleached sheds have a dull resonance and the difference between live antlers will be detected by deer. It is best to cut off the eye guard tines to protect yourself from accidental finger smashing. Also, practice by holding the antlers different ways until you achieve the desired results that sound most like deer meshing their antlers. Drill a hole near the base and tie the antlers together with an 18"-24" cord. This allows you to drape them over your shoulder while hunting so one hangs in front and one in back. Some hunters stain the antlers dark or camouflage them, while others, concerned with mistaken identification by another hunter, paint them orange. To keep their fresh, live tone, antlers can be soaked in water frequently during the season, or have a coating of linseed oil or wax applied to them. During the off season, store your rattling antlers where they will not dry excessively.

The location that you choose for rattling is extremely important. Set up in an area of scrapes combined with rubs where bucks, eager to breed, are most active. This is also the most likely location for a buck confrontation and the bucks will be focused on action from

Carry rattling antlers over shoulder to keep them from bumping together.

there. It is also feasible to rattle adjacent to a bedding area and lure a buck close enough to the edge for a shot.

If the peak of the rut in your area is mid November, use a sparring technique while hunting in early October since the bucks are still in bachelor groups. A sparring sequence may involve one initial clash of the antlers but is mainly a non-violent twisting and grinding together for 15-20 seconds at 15-20 minute intervals. Since it is mostly a pushing and shoving match, tickle or brush the tips of the tines together initially and then slowly rub the bases together firmly, simulating neck twisting. The bucks are not fighting, but only sparring to determine the strongest and most dominant. Since deer are becoming more wary of daytime rattling, you should introduce secondary sounds associated with bucks sparring. Thump the ground with an antler or the heel of your leather boot to imitate deer hooves struggling for balance. Kick leaves or shake a bush to simulate two large animals wrestling recklessly. This will help convince a mature buck to investigate, since he knows that no hunter would make noises like that in the woods. Occasional use of a grunt call can also be effective. The hunter must be very patient since not all deer rush in to become involved but may approach out of curiosity simply to watch. Early in the season one year, I sparred, waited, and then sparred again. After waiting for a while, I climbed from my tree stand and spooked a nice buck that had snuck in under my tree to watch the sparring contest and was concealed by the thick foliage. As far as I know that buck is still looking up into trees while walking down a path.

Hold rattling antlers for a tine mesh that is comfortable to you.

During pre-rut, the rival deer actions can become more violent, especially among equally sized competitive bucks. Different sized bucks will spar together, but usually only evenly matched bucks must fight to settle the order of dominance. There may be more than one clash, but the hunter must also use some common sense. For example: two 200 pound, four footed animals, cannot charge and retreat as quickly as the hunter slapping antlers together with wide arm swings. During this dominant

Bucks spar in late summer to determine order of dominance. Photo by Ted Rose

rattling sequence, a short antagonistic grunt, along with secondary noises like we used in sparring, is a good strategy. The meshing of the antlers should also be more jerky and violent. An actual fight could last for a hour or more but a few minutes of rattling will usually do the job, allowing an hour spacing between fights.

During the rut, when a buck finds a receptive doe, rattling will not interest him because he already has what he wants. Since the most dominant bucks select does first, the dominant rattling technique is most effective early on when territories are being challenged.

The final opportunity for rattling success occurs in the post rut period. Younger bucks, ready and eager to breed, or mature bucks frantically searching for late unbred does, can be drawn toward the hunter by sounds of a deer fight.

The best times of the day to rattle are early morning or late evening since deer are most active and less wary at those times. The secret is to find a buck that is in the proper frame of mind. The buck to doe ratio will also affect your results. If there are plenty of does for all the bucks without a fight, they will settle for what they have and avoid a confrontation. In other words, they will not approach the rattling sounds.

During my early rattling years, while bow hunting in mid November, I made a novice mistake. A young six-point buck checked the bedding area for a receptive doe about 50 yards from my tree stand, and then, turned and angled away. Thinking that I might bring him back, I rattled when he was about 200 yards down the trail but still in sight. At the sound of the meshing antlers, he stopped, flattened his ears, dropped his head and shoulders into a subordinate posture and quickly trotted away. If I had been more experienced, a few seductive doe grunts might have lured him back, but apparently he had recently been dominated by a larger buck and did not desire a repeat lesson.

A buck approaching your rattling site will invariably approach from downwind, looking for the combatants as he approaches. If you are hunting alone be absolutely sure that you are deodorized. Some deer scent lure might help bring the buck those final steps if you are archery hunting. Try some doe-in-heat on cotton balls in an elevated position for maximum airborne scent dispersion. If you are working with another hunter, the rattling, with associated sounds, can be done most effectively from the ground, while your partner is located in a tree stand 40-50 yards downwind.

Immediately stop rattling or grunting if the deer starts in your direction. Use these techniques only to bring animals back if they lose interest or to coax them into range if they are bypassing your stand.

In early October a few years ago, I raked and thrashed nearby brush with an antler while stomping and kicking in the dirt of a fresh primary scrape adjacent to a doe bedding area. Almost instantly, from about 600 yards downwind, a 140 class, ten-point materialized from a briar thicket. Slowly, but deliberately, with head held high, he approached his scrape trying to look west, into the suns dying rays, to see who the intruder was in his territory. As he crossed my entry trail from two hours earlier, the big buck side stepped toward the woods but remained in the field to better view the action at his scrape. As he approached the scrape with a stiff legged menacing stalk, the intruder shot him at a distance of 25 yards.

10-point came to investigate intruder at primary scrape.

Since rattling has become increasingly popular, more deer have been educated. A buck that has been fooled by a hunter, but escaped, will be suspicious of daytime rattling and will have a more cautious approach. For this reason, do not practice in your hunting area, but try an area where hunting is not permitted, such as a state park.

The two most important factors for successful rattling are the location where you set up and your patience while hunting.

You cannot unring a bell and you cannot unshoot a gun, so be certain of your target.

DEER SOUNDS IN THE FOREST

When is the best time to use which deer vocal under what circumstances? You can almost state, that if you will grunt anytime and you actually sound like a deer, then it is likely that a deer will come and investigate out of curiosity or social responsibility. This is especially true in the fall of the year when the message that a deer receives excites them into a reaction. Of course, if a hunter uses the correct communication, it will increase the chances that the animal he lures toward him will be a buck and that he will come in close enough for a proper shot into the vitals. A grunt may have several different meanings associated with various body postures and different circumstances. What we want to determine is the best voice imitation to use at the appropriate time.

Bucks voice warnings and challenges to others as the rut heats up. Photo by Ted Rose

Thanks to studies by wildlife researchers like Doctors Larry Marchinton, Tom Atkeson and Karl Miller from the University of Georgia, we have much more information for hunters. They recorded deer vocalizations and then separated them into categories to help differentiate the animal's intentions. From these researchers and others, it is possible to interpret various vocals and evaluate the most opportune time to try them in the field. The five types of calls that are normally imitated by hunters include: 1.) tending grunt 2.) attention or social grunt 3.) aggressive grunt 4.) bleat and 5.) doe grunt.

Presently, the most popular technique for bringing bucks close is the *tending grunt*. It is the mating sound of an aroused buck making choppy, guttural sounds similar to a hog and works well in the early rut. This sound involves a series of low pitched, loud, excited grunts about two seconds apart. This pleading communication lasts a little longer than the other grunts and can be up to 1 1/2 seconds long. The buck might make 10 such consecutive grunts in a 30 second time frame or he might provide a pattern such as 3 grunts, a several second pause, 3 grunts, another pause, and then 4 grunts, all in an excited exhibition of attention. This indicates the presence of an estrous doe, or at least that is the buck's conception. If you can watch the buck when you follow this routine and he reacts by raising his tail stiffly to a horizontal hold, you have the attention of his libido and he will probably circle downwind and head in. Unless you are trophy hunting, a common mistake is to use the most dominant sound that your call produces. For best results, you should use a medium voiced grunt. Even a dominant buck might use caution when he hears the voice of a really big buck. He might get hung up at 50 yards trying to get a visual of this big guy before making his move to reclaim his doe. On the other hand, he will be more apt to approach with aggressive behavior and less caution if he thinks a lesser buck is tending one of his does. That is the reaction that you want from the buck.

Since deer are very social in the fall, due to their breeding season, an *attention grunt* has great communication possibilities. This call can be used to stop a deer that is moving past and allow the opportunity for a standing shot. It is a single or double, gentle tone, medium volume friendly grunt that lasts 1/2 to 1 1/2 seconds long and should be spaced several minutes apart. This social call is most likely to seduce younger bucks 12 to 18 months old. These animals have been rejected by their mother and run off by dominant bucks as the breeding period begins. They are searching for friends and are often in strange surroundings trying to establish their own territories. This vulnerability makes them more willing to accept the company of any deer, including a stranger.

A deer is often cautious when answering to a grunt call and suspicious when no deer is visible. Photo by Ted Rose

When breeding possibilities approach and the intensities increase, more *aggressive* sounds are used by both bucks and does. This grunt is a higher pitched, short, sharp tone of only 1/4 second and is usually needed only once or twice. This sound is used as a final threat or warning by the dominant buck to other bucks, combined with hostile body language such as stiff legged walking, laid back ears and bristling hair. It is a good preliminary sound to make prior to dominant rattling or for emphasis during the fight. In addition, the grunt-snort or the grunt-snort-wheeze is one of the best indicators of a hot buck on a hot doe. The buck emits a short grunt on exhale, followed by a wheeze when he sucks air back in. This sound often accompanies his trotting cadence while in pursuit of an estrous doe and if properly imitated will bring other bucks running to try to get to the doe first. This combination of grunting and air hissing sounds is irresistible to a dominant buck.

When a buck has a doe in tow, a call to him has little value in an attempt to bring him close enough for a shot. He will steer the estrous doe away from any male competition. However, a doe with a buck might be fooled if you use a few fawn distress *bawls or bleats*. The call for help from a frightened or injured fawn is a loud, one second (or longer), wailing baaa type cry. Even if the doe does not recognize the voice as her own fawn, she may feel compelled to try and rescue the youngster. Her presence will probably bring the buck, interested in only the doe, following close behind. This fawn distress call seems to work best about a month or so prior to the rut, since, after the doe has weaned her fawns, she will be less responsive to cries for help.

Possibly the best enticement to a buck is a *doe grunt*. This short, soft, medium-high pitched grunt of a mature doe is exactly what all of the bucks are listening for. They would much rather connect with a girl deer than contest with another buck. Try this technique during the rutting period with several soft calls a few seconds apart.

Of course there are exceptions to every rule and I must share a mid-November experience with you. It was a damp, 45° morning, with a 5 mph stiff breeze. I was set up in a pine thicket downwind of a "no hunting", unfarmed, sidehill field, containing scattered briar patches and cedar trees. At daybreak, the grunts started from a location that I judged to be 500 yards away. It sounded like some kid just got his first grunt call and was trying to round up his hogs. About every 45 minutes, a series of 6 to 10 grunts broke the stillness. They ranged from 2 second pleading grunts, to medium length, high pitched grunts, to short, low, tending grunts with some even cut off in mid-grunt. It sounded like the kid was swinging his head from north to south, blowing with all he had. It was like nothing I had ever heard before. About mid-morning the fog broke, and with my binoculars I was surprised to see a young eight-point buck making advances on a less interested bedded doe.

Deer calling is quite often used by archery hunters where it is necessary to bring deer close enough for a sure shot. As an added benefit, the technique of calling can help keep you in a tree stand longer without getting impatient. Keep in mind that noise travels farther from an elevated perch and do not call too loudly. On a calm, still day, when calling is most effective, a deer can hear a call at 500 yards that a normal human ear can

Listening to tapes will help your imitation of whitetail vocals.

detect at 50 yards, or about ten times as far. For best results, you should carry several grunt calls for various deer voices. If you have been identified by a deer in the past while grunting, they can remember the voice and will avoid the area.

Most of us string our grunt call on a lanyard around our neck where it is quickly accessible. During archery season, be aware that this dangling projectile could get caught in your bow string on release, and not only throw your shot off, but also launch your call on a short, fast, journey around your head and into your face. Miles Keller suggested a good idea at a recent hunting seminar. Simply sew a camo pocket on your left jacket shoulder (for right handed shooters) and place your call in it while on stand. With only a head turn you can blow the call, leaving both of your hands free to hold your equipment.

On some days, deer tend to be less social and more hungry. After a long period of bad weather would be an example, and they are not very responsive at that time.

While working a deer, if the animal is looking toward you or showing attention, do not continue to call. They will pinpoint your location very accurately and could spot you as you move into shooting position. If they turn away, call again to arouse their curiosity or create a behavior that will bring them within range.

Finally, for your own safety, never use your grunt call to get the attention of another hunter.

The worn out doe emerging from the woods was overheard declaring . . . "I'll never do that again for two bucks!"

THE BUCKS STOP HERE

How many of you will admit, that as you sit in your tree stand, and time passes by, while your patience grows thin, you find yourself wishing that a big, old, monster, mossyhorn, record class buck would walk down the trail and stop broadside right in your shooting lane? Will it ever happen? No! My wish was never granted either. While I will admit that some good luck must accompany you to succeed, much of it you can create with application of experience and knowledge about whitetail deer. In order to successfully stay on stand and concentrate, a hunter must have the confidence to believe in his stand location.

You must decide ahead of time that, although a doe would be legal, this hunt is for a buck. You might even shoot a subordinate buck tomorrow but today the dominant buck is your goal as you wait on stand, mentally reviewing the information that you have gathered throughout the previous weeks. The rubs and scrapes that you located within your hunting area have brought you to this location today. Let's review the data.

The September brushing of bushes and small trees has been for the removal of dead velvet from the antlers. This fairly gentle but thorough rubbing may take a day or two to complete. In October, bucks will spar with each other and show aggressive behavior while making rubs on trees. This aggressive pre-rut behavior pumps up the bucks' neck while leaving scars on many woodland trees.

Rubs occur on small, especially aromatic trees like cedar, pine, maple or sumac. They are most noticeable about a month prior to the breeding period. These bare areas

Bucks shed the velvet membrane covering their antlers during the first week of September in the Northern United States. Photo by Ted Rose

Author inspects rub on large ash tree.

The height and size of a rub can indicate the maturity of a buck, like this high one on a cherry tree.

of wood are easily visible to hunters and other deer. Close inspection will not only reveal small scratches from antler bumps and stickler tines but you will also find forehead hair where the buck left his glandular secretion for identification. This serves as a warning to other bucks of a territory where trespass will not be tolerated and the intruder will be challenged.

Use the height of a rub, the size of the tree skinned and incidental damage to adjacent saplings and bushes to evaluate the size and antler maturity of the buck. If the main tree rubbed is 2"-3" in diameter or larger, with branches or bark shredded and ripped above your waist level, it is undoubtedly a good buck. If adjacent saplings have received damage from antler tines extending beyond the rubbed tree, you should be able to estimate antler length.

A line of rubs will indicate the direction that the buck was traveling from his security area, and it is likely that he will follow this same route again. If you find a couple of rubs in an area just inside the woods, it is probably a staging area initiated by a dominant buck. These multiple rubs are a result of the aggressive thrashing of a dominant buck as he sends a warning to intimidate lesser bucks that have entered the field with his does. The dominant buck, waiting for the cover of darkness before leaving the woods, is trying to frighten off any subordinate competition. A group of a dozen or so rubs in a thicket, some on large trees, confirm the presence of a mature buck and might indicate the site of his bedding area.

Scrapes begin appearing by early October and can be classified as incidental or important. That means they are either secondary or primary. Secondary scrapes, which usually appear first, include boundary activity and other impulsive type scrapes. These small scrapes are partially pawed areas along field edges or even along travel routes. They serve to warn other bucks that a dominant buck is in the area. Some may even be dug out to bare ground, but none have an overhanging branch, and they are not revisited with any predictable regularity. I inspect secondary scrapes only for any identifiable hoof prints.

Buck makes boundary scrape in field edge and drags antler tines through it. Photo by Ted Rose

Primary scrapes, on the other hand, can be part of a buck's routine and some of them can be valuable to the deer hunter. They are often a 3-4 feet long by 2-3 feet wide area of exposed ground, cleared of all debris and with a muddy textured surface. The buck's tracks along with his antler drag marks may appear in the scrape. These scrapes are located near the does bedding area

Buck making a primary scrape in soft earth. Photo by Ted Rose

or in a place where does frequent and are positioned where they will be obvious to willing does. All primary scrapes will have an overhanging branch 4 to 6 feet off of the ground above the scrape. This branch will be marked by the buck with his saliva containing individual pheromones and a distinctive sudoriferous secretion from between his antlers. His signature may be completed with additional rubbing of a discharge from his pre-orbital gland located in the front corner of his eyes. Not all primary scrapes are revisited as I have observed. I usually kick leaves into any primary scrape that I pass for the purpose of eliminating the ones that are not active and are not reopened. You would not want to disturb this sensitive area for forest deer or if it was a scrape that you intended to hunt near. To help cover human odors, I drip doe urine on the toe of my rubber boots prior to kicking leaves into the scrape. Some primary scrapes that I have covered in the middle of October have not been re-opened by mid-November, when the peak of the rut occurs in this area. If you find a primary scrape early, and in thick heavy cover, you may want to treat it differently because a trophy buck will scrape early and never intends to leave security cover to locate a mate. Since scrapes are made only by dominant bucks, the mature females will instinctively visit them prior to the breeding period in search of a suitable mate. Contact is made at the scrape and then the discreet breeding partners depart.

The best time to hunt an active primary scrape is a few days prior to the peak of the rut as does come into estrus and search for a buck. Also, the dominant buck instinctively knows that a heavy rainfall will obliterate his scent signature and he will run his scrape route to freshen his best scrapes immediately following the rain. When these two circumstances coincide, the combination can be deadly near the scrape. A buck will urinate into his scrape over his hocks, carrying scent from the tarsal glands on the inside of his legs to the ground. Freshening of his scrape includes this urinating procedure following removal, by pawing with his front feet, of any leaves or debris that have fallen or been blown into the scrape. Droppings may also be found in scrapes but are incidental to the breeding process.

Researchers report that mature does become active on the afternoon before they come into estrus. This is another opportune time to be on stand near a primary scrape as the doe deposits her scent. She then waits for the dominant buck to appear and hangs around for this love connection.

Receptive doe allows dominant buck to approach her as he prepares to breed. Photo by Ted Rose

Rutting activity increases as the temperature decreases. With everything else ready, a cooling period encourages increased activity from both sexes.

Keep in mind that bucks will revisit scrapes where they have had success with does. If a bachelor meets a "pretty woman" in a bar, this bar will become his favorite hang out and he will revisit it often with high hopes for another friendly encounter.

Since dominant bucks make scrapes, but subordinant bucks visit them, you should be aware that their approach may be distinguishable. If a lesser buck approaches with timidity or hunched into a subordinant apologetic posture, he is not the scrape buck but merely a hopeful visitor. The buck that boldly checks the scrape, in charge of his approach, is your dominant scrape maker.

Scrapes that seem to attract year-long attention with the necessary well chewed branches overhead are probably the community licking branch locations. This special branch is the deer's version of a year around hang out. Although I recognized these areas as continuous deer hot spots and hunted them as active primary scrapes, I did not categorize them as licking branches until reading an article by Bob McGuire of Johnson City, Tennessee. He accurately described what I had witnessed at several licking branch sites. The location of this branch, often where several trails intersect, is a worthy site for a good stand on both sides. The two stand locations give you the option for morning or evening hunts in addition to varying wind directions. Several bucks along with does will visit this location on a regular basis.

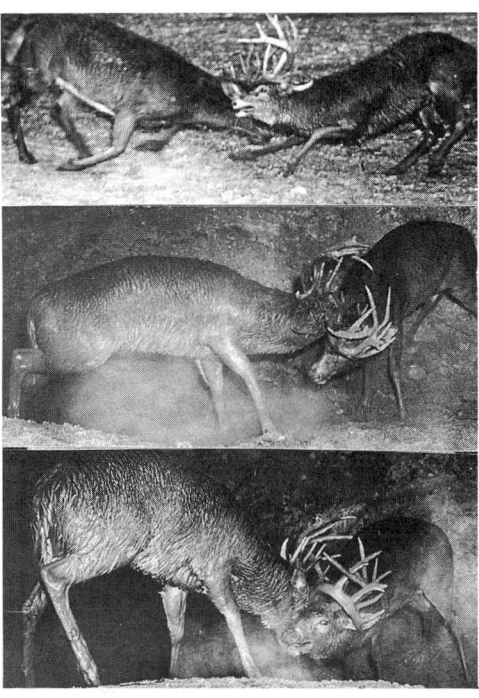

Fighting bucks occasionally get their antlers enmeshed.

A challenging contest began while bowhunting in early October during a heavy downpour. I had the opportunity for an open, broadside shot at a fine nine-point traveling in tandem with an eight-point. Due to my inexperience with the effect of heavy rain on my arrow, combined with an estimated range of almost 40 yards, I did not release the arrow. From that moment, I knew that I would hunt this buck for the rest of the season. The image of his high tines, slanting inward over his head were etched into my hunting mind.

Later in October, I found his active scrapes near the does bedding thicket along with several rubs. One scrape in particular caught my attention. It was in the same location as last years and the apple branch, about six feet above it, was chewed and hooked thoroughly. I knew that if I removed the branch, he would abandon the scrape immediately, but it was not in the vicinity of a good stand tree. I located a position at the woods edge to create a false or mock scrape where several trees would provide stand sites. It was about 100 yards from the primary scrape at the thicket. Several days later, during a light rainfall, I returned to the active primary scrape. Wearing rubber gloves and rubber boots, like a trapper, I clipped off the apple branch and moved it to its new location. A large scrape was fashioned under the re-hung branch and several ingredients were added to the fresh dirt. The most important, a doe-in-heat urine, was liberally applied. Additional 100% doe urine which I had also applied to my boots, leaving a trail from the original scrape, was sprinkled around the mock scrape as a curiosity scent. To excite a higher degree of recklessness into the original scrape maker, I added some buck urine to the area. My nine-point should then read another bucks intrusion into his breeding territory, plus a ready doe in the vicinity.

On the afternoon of November 13, I noted fresh activity in the mock scrape while dragging a doe-in-heat soaked rag to it so I dumped the rest of the bottle of this sex lure into the scrape. Nothing followed my drag or came to the scrape on this final evening of bow hunting. At dark, I relocated my portable stand to a better vantage point for a longer shot since the next day was opening day of the firearm season.

Entering the woods at 6 AM, I kicked some leaves into another primary scrape that I suspected belonged to my nine-point. Later inspection would show that he had re-opened this scrape enroute to the mock set up. I stayed far downwind of the mock scrape to eliminate any possible scent contamination. My stand, safely locked high in an ash tree, was waiting when I arrived and it did not take me long to re-insert the steps and climb back up. Now, with the mock scrape prepared and showing evidence of recent attendance, I confidently sat and waited for my buck.

It seemed like only a few moments before I realized that darkness had disappeared and legal shooting hours had arrived. The morning was perfect for an opener, with moderate temperatures and a faint west wind. Heavy dew covered every leaf and occasionally dripped to the ground when an unseen breeze stirred the mist. At about 9 AM, after very little shooting from nearby farms, a slight movement downwind of the mock scrape caught my eye. It was a phantom line, like a drifting spider web, but this one had antlers. Through the scope over my 50 caliber renegade muzzleloader, the swollen neck of the nine-point was visible between two trees and that was all I needed to bring him down. He had been checking his scrapes and was about 60 yards downwind of my scrape, looking for the estrous doe when I first spotted him. The dominant buck did not yet have a doe but aromatic evidence of his scrape activity filled the air as I approached him for the coup de grace.

9-point was caught checking scrape.

A broadhead should be so sharply honed that you can get cut just by looking at it.

Let us not take aim at another bowyer that opts for different equipment. Shai Nobel (author's brother) hunts with a scope mounted crossbow, while traditional archer, Brad Main, hunts successfully with longbow and self made cedar arrows.

CAN TOXOPHILITES BE DANGEROUS TO YOUR HEALTH?

They can if you are a whitetail deer! By definition, a toxophilite is a lover of the bow, or an archer. The unique feature of this sport is that very few bowyers are identically equipped.

Beginners should look for advice and guidance from a reliable archery pro shop. After determining whether your bow will be a longbow, recurve, compound or crossbow, the selection of the equipment (tackle) becomes a personal choice. When selecting a bow, never "dry fire" it, meaning, never release the string without an arrow nocked. It will damage limbs, pulley or string. Also, never pull an empty string back using a mechanical device in case it accidentally releases.

The arrow is the most critical item of tackle for an archer and the broadhead is the most important part of the arrow for the hunter. Arrow shafts can be aluminum, fiberglass, graphite or wood, with aluminum being by far the most widely used. Based on your draw length and the weight (pounds pull) of your bow, the arrow is selected. The arrow shaft stiffness, or spine, is the factor used for selection, so that your arrow is flexible enough to function properly. Use an arrow selection chart for this choice. The weight of the field point used for practice should match your broadhead weight and the fletching selection should provide proper stabilization for your arrow flight.

For fletchings, the lighter, natural feathers are more forgiving when clearing the sight window, but require more care than the durable plastic vanes. Straight fletchings may also offer better clearance but a couple of degrees of helical mounting will provide better arrow flight by recovering from release errors. Mounting the fletchings at a slight angle will cause the arrow to spin during flight and stabilize. Bright colored, dull finish fletchings and nock will help you follow arrow flight during your shot to better determine hit location more accurately. They are also helpful in finding your arrow after the shot. You might try blue fletchings for a good contrast with anything natural.

Broadheads are available with two to six cutting edges, while the three or four blade models are the most popular. I prefer blades at least .020" thick with a 1 1/4" diameter for maximum cutting area. Blades, sharp to the point, provide the maximum cutting edge while sharpened steel pointed models are popular with many hunters. The hunter has an almost endless choice of fixed blades, inserts or even blades that open on contact. Broadheads should be mounted on shafts 1" longer than your draw length to clear the riser. Check each broadhead alignment on the arrow shaft by spinning them with the point on a hard surface. If misalignment occurs, the arrow could wind plane, or glide off target and correction or replacement of the blade is necessary. Vented or cut-out type blades seem to perform best since they will not have a tendency to wind plane. For small game and some practice shooting, judo points or blunts can be used. To complete your arsenal of hunting points, stoppers are available to minimize penetration for hunting turkey or other small game, while barbed points are used for bowfishing.

Practicing with broadhead on 3D target helped David Jarboe have a successful hunting season.

Technology has outdone itself when it comes to the arrow rest. This simple shelf on which the arrow rests, allowing quiet drawing and shooting, has advanced from the edge of a native American's finger to overdraw channels allowing the arrow to be up to 5" shorter. Pay particular attention to this item of tackle and do not hesitate to upgrade your original purchase if a more durable product is marketed. Along with the rest usually comes an arrow holder, so that your finger is never used to hold the arrow nor sticking in the way of your broadhead at full draw. Two concerns of the holder are to insure that it is clear of your fletchings and noiseless during your draw.

Sights range from no sights for the instinctive shooter to a projected laser dot, and include bow scopes along with various configurations of sight pins and crosshairs. The most popular and reliable models are three or four adjustable pins on a fixed frame. Peep sights and/or kisser buttons mounted on the string are another alternate for improved accuracy by some archers.

Dave Cruser takes aim on a carp. Bowfishing requires fast reflexes and some instinctive shooting.

Bow silencing begins with strips of rubber, yarn or other material woven into the bowstring. Some of these materials are light enough to act as wind indicators while others may actually slow bowstring velocity. I had a cable friction squeak on my compound bow until a roller slide was installed on the cable guide. To further quiet your bow you may have to try heavier arrows, reduce your bow weight if you are shooting a compound, or even add a stabilizer to dampen vibrations. The addition of a stabilizer for bow balance, less recoil or noise reduction is common for target shooters but some bow hunters also use them, especially the shorter 6-16 ounce camo models. Hydraulic stabilizers are fast gaining in popularity.

Optional equipment such as brush guards, limb covers, torque compensators, specialized grips, bow sling or game tracking line may be selected to personalize your hunting bow.

The final piece of equipment that might attach to your bow is the quiver. While the bow quiver is the most popular model for hunting, due to convenience, back and hip models have regained popularity in recent years as some bowyers have reverted to recurve and longbows. Hunting quivers must hold arrows quietly while protecting the hunter from the broadhead edge.

From tabs for target shooters to three finger gloves for hunters, many of us have evolved to a mechanical release. It protects our fingers on heavy hunting bows and provides a smooth, more consistent, lower vibration release under various weather conditions. Shoot several releases before deciding which one to purchase. Be careful that it does not damage the serving with constant shooting.

Attach your camo, fleece armguard and you are now ready to set up your bow for tuning. On a recurve be sure to match the brace height with the manufacturers recommendation by twisting the string as required. On a compound, unless you have installed a non-stretch string, you should already be set up for tuning. Be sure that your bow is at zero tiller. This means that the distance of the string to the point where the limb meets the riser on both the upper and lower limb is equal.

Initially, the cushion plunger should be set so that the center line of the arrow is about 1/16" outside of the bowstring. The cushion plunger is a spring loaded device called a berger button, after its designer Victor Berger, and is installed to decrease shaft vibration. Begin with the bottom of your nocking point about 3/8" above the top of the rest.

Tuning your bow for speed and accuracy will include adjustments for porpoising, fishtailing and clearance. All equipment should be securely attached prior to tuning and any equipment variations may require re-tuning for best performance.

Porpoising is vertical wobble and is caused by the nocking point being too high or low. This motion must be corrected before any other tuning can occur. Using three fletched and three unfletched arrows, shoot all six at a range of about 15 yards with an identical sight picture. If your bare shafts group higher than the fletched ones, raise the nocking point. If the bare shafts plane down below the fletched shafts, move the nocking point down. When all arrows impact at the same elevation, record this measurement, tighten the nocking point and consider attaching a second nocking point above it to insure that the first one remains in place.

The next adjustment is to eliminate fishtailing, or excessive horizontal flex of the arrow. Shoot three bare arrows and three fletched arrows into a short range target as before. For right handed archers, if the group of bare arrows centers to the left of your fletched shots, you can either move the arrow in toward the bow or decrease the spring pressure on the plunger. If the unfletched arrows group to the right of your fletched shots, move the rest out from the bow or increase plunger spring tension. Left-handed archers should make their adjustments opposite to the above. Paper tuning, which involves close range shooting through paper in a frame, shows slots in lieu of perfect holes and is also a successful and quick way to tune your bow.

Finally, check for arrow clearance by spraying or dusting talcum powder or dry deodorant on the arrow rest, sight window area and back quarter of the arrow, including the fletchings. After a shot, check the arrow and sight window for any drag marks. Contact with the bow can usually be eliminated by moving the Berger button pressure point further out and then re-tuning for fishtailing. Further contact could require a change in arrow spine or a weight adjustment if you are tuning a compound bow. If the nock end of the arrow drags the far side of the bow, a stiffer shaft may be required, but contact with the near side of the bow indicates that the shaft is too stiff. To obtain clearance from my spring rest I had to rotate all of my arrow nocks about 4° off of perpendicular with the cock vane.

Check again for cable or string noise or loose equipment vibration. Adhesive moleskin can be used to cover the sight window, dampening noise from accidental arrow contact.

To sight-in your bow, carefully measure off the distances that you will use to set your sights. Adjust sight in the direction of error or "follow the arrow." If you shoot low, lower your sight to raise the bow. If shooting to the right, adjust sight to the right to correct the error. Be sure that your back muscles are loosened up prior to any shooting to eliminate back strain. Try leaning your back or arm against a building or tree for stability as a bench rest while sighting-in.

After you have developed your individual style and have some consistency in arrow groups, practice various positions such as sitting, kneeling, off balance leaning positions, shooting around bushes or under tree limbs. Shoot from your blind or tree stand, including shots around the tree. While practicing, learn to estimate distances. A rangefinder is useful for verifying distances and also valuable when you arrive on your hunting stand to check possible shot distances. Since you can estimate short distances more accurately, pick a spot half way to the target, estimate the distance and then double it. This procedure of twice half the distance is also effective for gun hunting estimates.

Woodchucks are vigilant, providing excellent stalking and shooting practice.

Simulate hunting conditions by slowly raising the bow and extending your arm. Hold this position while you slowly draw arrow to your anchor point. A belt mounted bow holder works great for taking strain off of your bow arm while on stand or stalking.

The bow should pull against the center of the Y formed between the thumb and the index finger of your bowhand. If your grip is loose, you could lose the bow after your release. However, if you grip the bow too tightly, your wrist could turn outward on release, causing errant arrow flight low and to that side. A wrist strap will eliminate any concern about dropping the bow and allow a grip-free release.

As hunting season approaches, shoot only one arrow from each position and study each shot. Insert and check broadheads on your hunting arrows by shooting each one. You will need to make slight adjustments to your sights when you switch to broadheads.

The two most important factors for a clean kill are arrow placement and a razor sharp broadhead.

If you shotgun (group shoot) a covey of quail, instead of selecting a single, you will more than likely miss. If you shoot at a deer, instead of aiming at a specific spot on that deer, which will allow penetration to the vitals, you will likewise probably be unhappy with the results. Concentrate on an exact aiming point during practice and this habit will transfer to hunting, teaching you to pick the spot that you intend to place your broadhead.

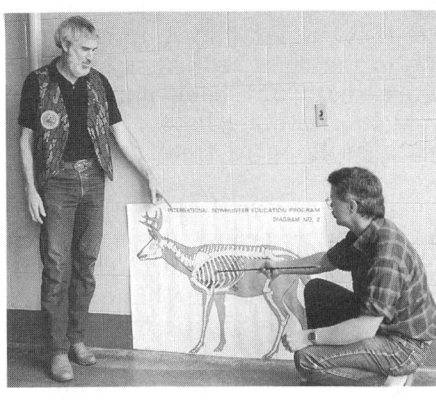

Dale Day shows Bowhunter Education Instructor Nobel that he would shoot for center of lungs.

Properly sharpening a broadhead is a new assignment to most of us. We can sharpen a knife to adequately field dress, skin, flesh a deer hide or even cape out a trophy head, but that is not enough. Sharpening the broadhead is a step beyond. After your broadhead is sharpened with a file, steel or stone, and all burrs removed from the cutting edge, it must be honed. This polishing is done by stropping the broadhead like a barber hones a straight razor. A coating of brasso or other very fine grit compound on the leather will promote honing as you back-drag your blade over it several times.

A bullet kills by shock, transferring it's energy to the game, but an arrow kills by producing maximum hemorrhaging, while transferring as little energy as possible. As an example, a scratch from a barbed wire fence is deep and painful, with great tissue damage, but almost no bleeding, while a slight nick with a razor while shaving is shallow, without pain, but it bleeds profusely and continuously. The greater tissue damage results in faster blood clotting which is undesirable for an arrow shot. The tiny muscles in blood vessels or artery walls will stretch out of the path of a dull blade but will sever cleanly when cut by a razor edge, resulting in internal hemorrhaging. Check your honed broadhead by gently sliding it over a rubber band stretched between your fingers. It should cut easily. To maintain razor sharp broadheads during hunting season, you will need to rehone them after a few weeks of rubbing in the quiver and oxidizing in the weather.

Many hunters, who have spent hours practicing, neglect to continue shooting during the season. Not only do your shooting muscles lose their tone but your timing is also affected. When you come out of the woods during daylight hours, shoot a few target arrows to keep in practice. At the least, pull your bow back beyond your anchor point twenty times whenever you pick it up.

Hundreds of hours of practice and hunting is reduced to a few seconds or less of arrow flight, so the bowyer must be totally prepared. Correct tackle selection, good practice habits, concentration on your exact point of aim and a razor sharp broadhead are requirements for responsible toxophilites.

You must draw your arrow excruciatingly slowly for a hunter in a hurry.

GET HIGH TO HUNT WHITETAILS

Never in my 40 years of deer hunting have I changed tactics with so much success. My new strategy is based on comments from speakers at several recent state deer hunting seminars combined with knowledge gained from teaching bowhunter education classes. Miles Keller urged "no scent hunting" for best results. Russell Thornberry described the cross section of a deer's vitals as 18 3/4" high by 18 1/2" wide, or almost square. Russell Hull suggested that sooner or later deer will visit their refrigerator, so this is the best place to wait for them. However, the major influence came from a speaker at the State Deer Classic. At first, I thought he was bragging or exaggerating when he claimed to set his stand 30 to 40 feet high. I even talked with him in his booth after the lecture to confirm his statement.

Simply stated: Would you shoot a deer if you had a 12 yard clear shot, the deer did not smell you, and you could move to draw your bow without being detected? When you realize that 36 feet is only 12 yards and that your arrow travels in an almost straight line, you will grasp the advantages as I finally did.

Tree selection is important to allow a clear shot, and some summer limb trimming will undoubtedly be required to open up several shooting lanes. Even a lone tall tree in a fence row can now be used for a stand location. Incidently, this high stand selection on windy days is not suitable, due to excessive tree motion.

Do not take this height casually, both for your sake and that of the deer. During target practice, you will notice the importance of maintaining the angle between your bow arm and body at about 90°. You must bend at the waist to achieve this angle and a secure safety belt, or harness, is

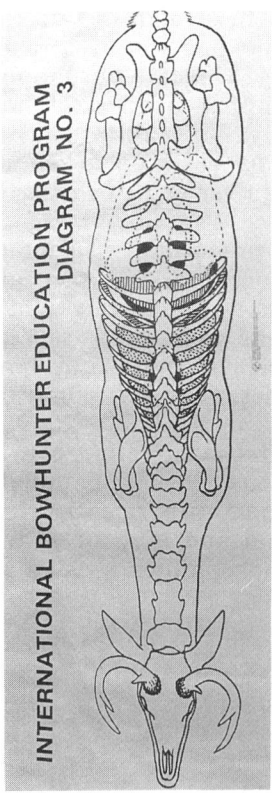

Note that the lungs are centered behind the front shoulder bulge.

mandatory. It is also critical to know the exact location of the deer vitals from above and the angle of entry behind the front shoulders so your arrow penetrates for a clean kill.

During the week prior to opening day, I spent each morning and evening slowly walking and glassing deer in my hunting area. The season opened that year on October first, with the bucks still in bachelor groups, so I concentrated my scouting on a group of three, including a spike, a 7-point and an 8-point. They were using two different bedding areas, although they would usually swing by the red oak trees prior to retiring for the day. This season the mast from the red oak was superior to the white oak crop in our area. By observing from a distance, I could easily see which red oak the deer favored and therefore selected a tall ash near the trail that led toward it.

On opening morning, with great confidence, I slipped into my tree stand long before daylight. That year, by doubling my previous stand height, I found myself seated about 33 feet above the ground. As anticipated, at 7:55 AM, the three bucks, in single file, entered the woods below, but an unforeseen event had altered their route. The farmer had harvested soybeans during the night causing the deer to detour to a different trail and they passed safely, 60 yards from my stand. Disappointed, knowing that my opportunity had passed, I watched as they fed around the red oak tree, hurried past another oak and disappeared into the tangle of their bedding area. Although in my heart the hunt was over, I remained dutifully in my tree for a few more hours and was rewarded by visits from several doe seeking acorns. Close observation of deer activity is normally exciting to me, but on that day it was a let down.

That evening, I corrected my mistake of trail sitting and went right to the source of the attraction. A river birch directly adjacent to the red oak was more slender than desired but it allowed me to attach my stand about

Screw-in steps and strap-on steps are installed using safety belt.

30 feet high, with a clear shot to one side of the big oak. As I walked under the oak for the first time, I observed that the ground was literally torn up from the sharp hooves of the acorn hunters. No deer visited the oak while I was waiting on stand that evening, so I locked it to the tree for the night.

From my stand at daybreak the next morning I spotted movement in the cut soybean field, and with my binocs, identified the three bucks as they circled and playfully sparred with each other. As they moved and continued sparring, I suddenly realized that they intended bypassing my location and heading for the bedding thicket. Grabbing my call, I softly voiced a doe communication grunt to remind the bucks of the waiting acorns.

From 200 yards away, the spike buck, followed by the 7-point, turned toward the oak tree. The eight-point, who was destined to be in my photographs later in the season, continued on to his bed. With no idea that he was about to move one step up the dominance ladder, the spike led the way directly below my stand without detecting my presence. While the 7-point slowly walked under my stand, I completed my draw unobserved. Setting my sight pin an inch off of the spine and directly behind the front shoulder bulge, I followed the buck for a few more steps until I was certain that the arrow would enter his body at the correct angle. Upon release, I caught a quick glimpse as the orange and red plastic vanes disappeared at the exact point of aim.

After a suitable wait, I retrieved the blood covered arrow and started following the trail. With an exit wound on the underside of the deer, the resulting blood trail made tracking easier. Even though the honed broadhead had just nicked the heart, one lung had completely collapsed and the trail led about 130 yards to the

Somebody else gets high with 22 steps, but it sure is ugly.

magnificent buck.

Although it may be uncomfortable at first, up there in nose bleed territory, this elevated perch is unbelievable, and you will definitely achieve a hunting high with a successful sure shot.

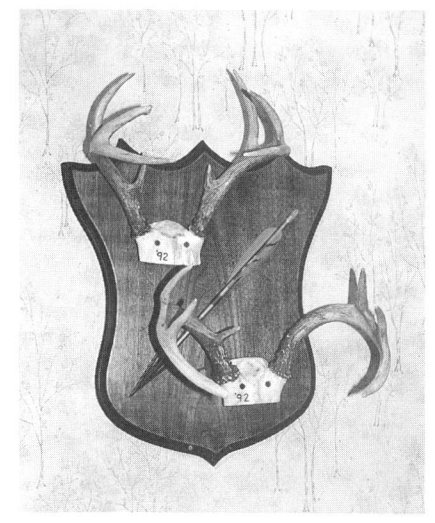

An exciting year!

Author with 7-point.

Keep in mind that a whitetail is a deer full time, while we are only part time hunters.

DOE SCENT DIVERSION

Both doe approaching stand.

For several evenings, I patterned two does near dark as they left their bedding area in a dense thicket and entered a field to feed. It was archery season and our legal hunting hours extended to one half hour after sunset. My problem was trying to get into position for a shot. Only one tree large enough for my tree stand was located close enough to the trail for a clear shot. Not only was this tree located straight ahead of the trail, on a bend, but it was also very short, and I knew that any move to draw my compound bow would be detected by the deer on the trail. What I needed was a way to stop the doe in a shooting lane with her eyes diverted from the tree and her body turned sideways for a broadside shot.

My strategy for the mid-October hunt was simple, but I had to wait two days for an evening with a light southwest crosswind. Then, clad in rubber boots and gloves, I carefully walked alongside the trail 15 yards from the tree to a point directly in line with my shooting lane. On the trail, and for several feet perpendicular to the trail, in the grass along both sides, I generously eyedropped 100% doe urine. Backing to the tree I quietly attached my stand about six feet off the ground in the only accessible location that the tree offered.

In full camouflage, including face mask, I sat, silently waiting for sunset and the hungry deer. I had not waited long when the first pair of ears appeared along the trail headed in my direction. Immediately my heart started pounding with excitement and my breathing got choppy as I watched the two does slowly approach. I knew that I had to be calm for a steady shot but my hand was already trembling in anticipation. It is amazing how slowly deer can walk, stopping frequently, when they are coming into range, and legal shooting light is rapidly waning. Without moving my head, I let my eyes purposely review my equipment, hoping to take my mind off the approaching deer and calm down. The honed broadhead was securely nocked and the arrow holder had my XX-75 Easton camo #2216 firmly snugged onto its wire spring rest. This final check of the gear increased my confidence and somehow quieted me down. Now, I was ready.

Finally, the lead doe reached the line of doe urine crossing her trail. she stopped and dropped her head to investigate this fresh scent. My grip tightened on the bow as the second doe swung her head to the side for a quick browse and I silently came to half draw. Two of my planned steps had succeeded. Now, all I needed was for my quarry to follow her nose to one side or the other. Her tail twitched as her head jerked back up one more time while she nervously surveyed the trail ahead looking past the camo figure motionless in the tree. As her nose returned to the deposited scent, her feet led her broadside. The second doe, bored with the delay, looked for more browse as I came to full draw and anchored. It was the ideal set-up at 15 yards and the arrow passed through both lungs before poking into the ground on the far side of the deer. She instantly whirled at the sound of the bowstring and retreated down her back trail

Release when near leg moves forward, exposing vitals.

Author with doe.

out of sight. After a 30 minute wait, I retrieved the arrow, covered with pink, frothy blood and followed the trail. The doe had traveled only 80 yards before finally dropping about 10 yards off the trail.

My strategy had worked. The doe scent had done its job by stopping the deer, diverting her eyes and getting her to turn broadside in the trail. That would not be my last time to use this successful tactic for deer hunting. Try it where you have an active trail and you want a deer to stop in a specific location while allowing you to draw your bow unnoticed.

Gun control is the art of being able to hit the bullseye.

SMOKEPOLES AND OTHER HUNTING ARMS

Since this is a hunting book and not a gun book, only a few comments will be directed toward the whitetail hunter's choice of gun or ammunition. The guns that are used to hunt whitetail deer include handguns, shotguns, centerfire rifles and muzzleloaders.

The most difficult of all firearms to master proficiently enough to hunt is the handgun. It requires constant practice to maintain shooting discipline. You should select your maximum load resulting in a recoil energy that is not unpleasant to shoot. With this in mind, many handgunners opt for the lighter but faster loads, which have less recoil and less drop but adequate energy for their limited ranges.

Shotguns have been used for years to hunt whitetails in their natural habitat of brushy river bottoms and thick woodlots. Buckshot is legal for deer in many states with some size restrictions, but today, slugs are most widely used. The accuracy of shotguns shooting slugs, in many respects, is equal to hunting with a centerfire rifle at ranges up to 100 yards. In the case of shotgun hunting, both the firearm and the ammunition have greatly improved in recent years. Now, better sights and scopes have given the newest shotgun set-ups a high shooting status. The rifled slug barrel, although not legal in all locales, has improved accuracy significantly over the smoothbore shotgun. First, an interchangeable rifled barrel was available, and now firearm manufacturers make a deer hunter's shotgun with a rifled barrel.

Shotgun Hunter!

Ever since the first Brenneke slug was introduced in Germany circa 1898, many variations have been developed for the modern shotgun hunter. Round "pumpkin balls" were displaced in the 1930's by the American inventor Foster who designed the slug with a heavy nose and hollow base. These slugs, although rifled, were used in smoothbore shotguns with fair results. Rifled slugs for a 12 gauge chambered for 2 3/4" shells can be either 1 ounce or 1 1/4 ounce, and for the past ten years they have competed with the 12 gauge, one ounce, 50 caliber sabot slug. The sabot slugs are designed to be used in rifled barrels or rifled choke tubes only. Slugs vary in diameter based on the manufacturer. For example: Remington slugs have the smallest diameter, with Federal slightly larger and Winchester largest. Logically, a full choke barrel might shoot a smaller slug like the Remington best, while rifled, open cylinder equipment might have better accuracy with the Winchester rifled slug or a sabot slug. You will need to spend some time on the range to decide the best load for your shotgun.

For centerfire rifle loads, manufacturers recommend 1000 to 1200 ft-lbs of energy as a lethal load for whitetail deer. With this in mind, many deer hunters select a rifle that can also be loaded for larger game and downsized for varmint hunting. Be prudent in this choice, so that you do not compromise your deer rifle, although it is excellent practice to use your deer rifle for varmint hunting. Record the number of clicks that you adjust your scope for the different loads, and prior to sighting-in for deer season, return the scope to the original setting. A variable scope, which is now engineered to remain on center at various powers, will provide the versatility that you desire.

Deer hunting with a muzzleloader, or smokepole, is a fast growing technique for two main reasons. There is greater reliability based on new technology and most states have extended hunting seasons for the primitive firearm. Deer hunting calibers include 45, 50, 54 and occasionally a big bore 58, with the 50 caliber being the most common. The Hornady ballistician, Bob Palmer advises that a minimum energy of 850 to 900 ft-lbs is recommended for whitetail muzzleloading arms. This is a lower striking energy than centerfire rifles due mainly to the larger diameter of the muzzleloading projectile. Ignition can be flintlock for the most primitive hunters or caplock (percussion) for the rest of us. To help insure firing, some manufacturers are breaking tradition with in-line ignition. Other shooter options include a modified nipple to receive centerfire primers in lieu of a number 11 cap. Many muzzleloaders come equipped with a second trigger or set trigger. This is great for sighting-in your gun or target shooting but is not necessary for a hunting situation.

More important to the hunter is the longer rifle barrel and especially the rifling twist. The faster the twist, the better the rifle shoots elongated bullets. If your rifling produces one twist in 60-66 inches, the gun is best suited to the slower turning of a round ball. The round ball is lighter, with less recoil, cheaper to shoot, and will drop less, so it also makes an excellent target load. If the twist is fast, so that the projectile will rotate once in 24-32 inches, it will impart the spin required to stabilize conical bullets. A twist of 1 in 48 inches would be suited for either projectile. Long barrels, and especially large octagonals, wide across the flats, can have internal stress that will affect bullet accuracy with temperature variations. A friend, that was an experienced shooter, missed a deer while we were hunting in 10° weather by shooting under it. Returning to camp he shot three rounds, with the second and third each rising about six inches. The next summer he put his muzzleloader into his freezer and shot it while still cold, only to find that it hit 12" low at 60 yards on the first shot.

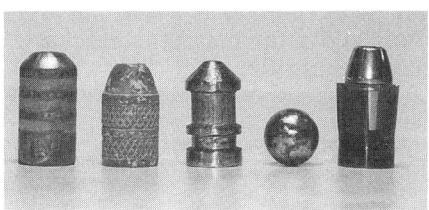

Common 50 caliber loads; 470gr prelubed T/C maxi hunter; 410gr prelubed Buffalo bullet; 370gr maxi hunter; 175gr, .490 round lead ball and 240gr Hornady 44 cal J.H.P. with sabot.

Whether your gun shoots a ball, elongated slug or sabot projectile, the powder charge must now be varied to obtain your most accurate group. If you start with one grain per caliber, your 50 caliber can be charged with 50 grains of black powder or Pyrodex. Calibers larger than 50 use FFg size while the 45 uses the smaller FFFg black powder and the 50 caliber can be loaded with either one. Pyrodex users should purchase R/S Pyrodex designed for use in Rifles/Shotguns. Pyrodex requires less cleaning than black powder and absorbs less moisture but requires a hotter spark to ignite. Smokeless powders should never be used in muzzleloading firearms. As more powder is added to your charge, in 5 grain increments, more velocity is imparted to the projectile. Various thicknesses of patches are used with balls to provide tight contact with the rifling. With a conical bullet or the sabot, the base expands on firing to fill the grooves and follow the rifling twist. Too much powder and therefore too high a velocity will cause the projectile to strip the rifling, allowing gases to blow by and you will lose accuracy. When this scattering of shots occurs, reduce your charge by 5 grains and you will have achieved your maximum powder load for that round. Mark your ramrod for this depth so you can verify that your muzzleloader is properly charged with the maximum hunting load. Swab the bore between shots for maximum accuracy. Some shooters use rubbing alcohol to clean powder residue. A second patch, seated on the powder prior to loading the patch/ball, might minimize some of this gas blow-by. Use only washed cotton material for patches since synthetic materials and additives can melt or cause fouling. You must maintain consistency while seating the bullet firmly onto the powder. Be sure that you do not leave a gap between the bullet and powder and do not beat the load with the ramrod, since it can distort or scar the front end of the projectile affecting accuracy.

Muzzleloading produces corrosive salts and your rifle must be thoroughly cleaned after shooting. Use very hot soapy water to remove greasy deposits. Use a base solution to neutralize any acidic salts, wire brush and then swab dry. Oil inside of barrel prior to storage. Keep in mind that black powder can increase in strength with age and old guns may still be charged, consequently they should be handled carefully.

A friend, Larry Lawson, shot this world record 187 1/8" buck with muzzleloader. Photo by Ted Rose

For hunting, after carefully loading your gun, place electrical tape over the muzzle to keep moisture and debris out. Next, measure a few extra charges into speed loader containers to carry in your possibles bag. You will also need a bullet starter and a capper for convenience. Most hunters carry the capper on a string around their neck where it is quickly accessible, along with a safety pin small enough to clear the nipple hole. Tools for breech or drum cleaning, a nipple wrench, spare nipple, patch puller, pipe cleaners and spare cleaning patches are all good ideas to have in your possibles bag.

Although the modern muzzleloaders have extremely reliable ignition systems, some unforeseen blunders can still occur. Once, in the early years, I thumbed back the hammer on a nice buck, set the trigger and squeezed off the shot. The only loud sound in the woods was the hammer striking the naked nipple. I had apparently knocked the cap off the nipple while cocking the hammer. Although his face was partially hidden from view, I could have sworn that the buck was wearing a wry smirk as he bounded off. He had bested the inept hunter that day.

Buck in velvet. Photo by Ted Rose

If people concentrated on the really important things in life, there would be a shortage of fishing poles and sporting guns.

THE BEST TIME TO SQUEEZE THE TRIGGER

The best moment to shoot a deer involves many variables, but mainly reflects back to gun selection and the personal marksmanship of the hunter.

Most firearms are selected based on hunting terrain and game laws. What guns are legal where you hunt and what equipment gives you the best advantage? Select a legal firearm, with equipment you can afford, and plan on becoming familiar with every aspect of this gun including sights and various ammunition. If your gun kicks hard or does not fit you well, trade it or sell it. Life is too short for a poorly fitted gun and so is hunting season with the opportunity for a shot. Factory guns are built for average size people and most of us nimrods are just not that average.

Prior to practicing with your equipment, the gun should be properly sighted-in. A hunter's responsibility to the deer dictates that you never ever take a gun hunting unless you have at least sighted it in yourself. Be sure to wear eye and ear protection when you do this. For the ultimate ear protection, wear both plugs and muffs. This will almost completely eliminate shooting noise and somehow seems to lessen the objectionable recoil felt from your gun. Place cushioning material between the butt plate and your shoulder on long guns to absorb some of the kick if you need to. Keep in mind that proper positioning of your gun

Sight-in rifle prior to practicing.

can lessen impact felt by your shoulder. This is especially true when shooting from a bench or table rest during sighting-in, when your body is not free to absorb the recoil. While using the bench rest and sand bags for sighting-in, shoot with the forearm and barrel unrestricted, allowing the gun to have full freedom to recoil. To adjust open sights, the rear sight should follow the direction of correction. Raise the rear sight to make the gun shoot higher and move it to the left to shoot further to the left.

An excellent practice method used by competitive shooters is described by Jim Carmichel in a 1981 *Outdoor Life* article. He recommends a dry firing technique. Be very sure that you use unloaded cartridge(s) in your firearm. You can learn to call your shot after you squeeze the trigger, with inexpensive, no recoil, no muzzle blast firing. If you are jerking the trigger or flinching, this practice will demonstrate these tendencies and allow you to smooth them out prior to shooting. Concentrate on a careful, steady squeeze of the trigger. If you do not s-q-u-e-e-z-e the trigger, but instead, suddenly jerk it, you are what you have done and the result will probably be a missed shot, or worse, a poor shot placement.

There is no substitute for familiarity with your equipment and the marksmanship ability that comes from practice. Be sure that you vary distances, positions and angles to the target. If you plan to hunt from a treestand, practice some 20 and 50 yard shots with your stand at a typical hunting height. On the ground, try some offhand shots at different distances to establish your personal limit of ability. Next, use a tree to steady your aim while standing. Be sure that the gun is not touching the tree when you shoot, but use your hand or arm for support. Sit at the base of a tree on your hotseat if this is a typical hunting position and shoot at various angles, especially straight ahead. Believe me, that is a very typical location for a deer to appear and it provides a difficult gun position for a steady shot. For handgunners, the most efficient field position is a braced sitting position using both hands to steady the gun. Both arms should be fully extended, braced on the inside of the knees, with the shooters back against a solid support, if possible.

It helps to target practice with an outline of the game animal so you can learn to shoot at the vitals and not toward the center of a bullseye. Another good idea is to cut actual game pictures out of magazines or use old wildlife calendars for practice targets. They are great at

Using a .22 caliber, Elton Beard shoots at calendar animal pictures for placement practice.

close range with a 22 caliber for simulating shot placement.

Shooting uphill or downhill lessons the gravitational influence and causes the bullet to hit high. The greatest gravitational influence is in the horizontal plane. A vertical shot, for example, would show no gravitational affect to bullet line of flight. Also, on downhill shots, the elevated effect tends to make the animal look smaller and often they are judged to be further away causing an even higher shot placement. Example: a 150 grain, 30-06 at 60° up or down will hit 4 1/2" above the line of sight at 200 yards.

Mental preparation is the final plateau of practicing. Even veteran hunters can get uncontrolled breathing and shaking with a fantastic rush of excitement caused by an approaching deer. With practice and confidence, all of your energies and abilities will become instinctive at the moment you concentrate on your shot. You have achieved your goal of practice when you can shoot as well at deer as you do at a target.

Now, let's go hunting! Always make one criteria your highest priority while hunting. Be sure that you make absolute positive identification of the game before you shoot. Remember, once the bullet has been shot, it can never be called back. With the one exception, I have always believed that hunters should set a goal to minimize meat damage when gun shooting deer. They should do everything within their power, including knowledge of their firearm and the location of the game's vitals. The one exception would be your very first deer. Just get it!

Naturally all hunters hope to get a clear, standing, broadside shot at the distance that they zeroed in their gun. Since this rarely happens, we must be prepared to take the best available shot the instant it is offered.

If a legal deer walks under your stand, you will be glad that you spent extra time practicing various distances and elevations. Now, if you desire, you can confidently make that 20 yard head shot. Along these same lines, if your equipment is capable of a 150 yard shot, and an incredible buck is standing at that distance broadside, daring you to measure his rack, you will appreciate the range time and the ammunition that you spent prior to the hunt. Set your sights to hit one third of the way up the body above the front leg.

Another popular aim point is a spine shot in the neck, especially when a close shot is offered. The reason that some hunters do not take this shot is because they know the bullet will destroy some neck meat in the impact area. Also, a deer can move his neck very quickly, causing a complete miss or pass through damage. If the pass through injury is to the windpipe for example, the hunter may not recover the animal although the shot could prove to be fatal.

A lethal shot on a deer moving straight away must be

centered exactly and is more luck than anything. A shot slightly off center, in the ham, can allow the deer to run for miles before dropping, leaving very little blood to trail. Quartering away shots provide a better target and can be made with the bullet entering the chest cavity from just behind the rib cage.

When you have the opportunity to shoot a moving deer broadside, forget all that you learned in shotgun class, even if you hold a shotgun in your hands. Think single projectile. Find a clear space between the trees on the trail ahead and hold for the deer to walk or run into your sight picture. Since most shots are made within 50 yards, the deer will only travel a few inches before your bullet finds it. At full tilt, it may go 6" while the bullet is in the air. In any case, the sights should be on the body of the deer with no lead. At 100 yards a walking deer may cover a foot, so the sight should be on the front of the chest to put your shot into the vitals. If running at 100 yards, you will need some daylight between the deer and your sights depending on the firearm being used. Knowledge of your ammunition ballistics is essential for this difficult shot.

Neck shot Sitka blacktail doe taken by author on Kodiak Island, Alaska.

When you kill a deer, make sure that it is dead. Approach from behind. Check to be sure that the eyes are open and the muscles are 100% relaxed. If the deer is squinting its eye, or if it flinches when an eye is touched, it is not dead and the hunter should immediately shoot it again, preferably in the head or heart.

The best shot may not initially be obvious, but hunting experience and patience, combined with knowledge of deer behavior will guide you. After first insuring yourself of proper game identification, determine when the deer will be within your personal range for a clear shot at its vital organs, and make your first shot count.

Wait for this undisturbed buck to turn, offering a clear shot at vitals. Photo by Richard Fields, I.D.N.R.

A hunter's degree of motion is inversely proportional to the number of deer to come within range.

Deer will look up into treestand if they detect motion or hear foreign noise. Photo by Ted Rose

TREESTANDS I HAVE KNOWN

At an early hunting age, stands on the ground never seemed to provide me with an adequate view of the surrounding terrain, especially if I decided to sit down. This hunting criteria led me either to small valleys overlooking active trails or up into the tree branches. You know that natural perches on tree branches were the first type of tree stand used and are still the best.

Tree stands are desirable for three main reasons. The hunter has a better view, his scent is above the animal and slight motions are usually not detected from below. Maybe even more important than these three logical reasons is the fact that it keeps you stationary for a longer period.

Most old timers, myself included, started with a crotch board tied into tree forks before making or purchasing their first portable tree stand.

If you decide to hunt from an elevated stand, put some thought into your typical hunting situation before making an investment. For example: if you normally have to haul your stand a long way, a lighter weight model of 11 pounds or lighter might be best. If most of your trees are straight with no limbs, a climber or some type of climbing steps will be required. However, if you hunt mostly in a thicket or a swamp, a self supporting type would be your best choice. If your hunts are short distances from your vehicle, a ladder stand with a platform on top might make a good arrangement. They are easy to install and climb while providing the hunter with a height advantage in thick cover. I have used them successfully set up on the backside of large trees in thick ground cover tangles. Try some stands used by other hunters that you know and shoot a few practice shots from each one as a test. Look for a sturdy one that fits your needs and that you feel comfortable in. Compare various manufactured stands that meet your conditions, and then buy the best that you can afford. You can often get a good used stand at a lower price. Many stands now have a seat and they should properly be called sits, since that is what you do most of the time. The taller seats which are about two feet high will be more comfortable. The method of attachment of the stand to the tree is important. A rubber coated chain is relatively indestructible and it also provides you with a reliable device for locking your stand in the tree during your absence. Some hunters will build a permanent stand in a tree along a trail used for many years by deer. If you own the woods and that is the only place where you hunt, this may provide all that is necessary.

"Old Timer" installing crotch board.

Select your stand sites based on location and position. Location is determined by deer activity such as their food source or bedding area, while position is determined by wind direction and time of day. When selecting a tree for a stand, stay away from wild cherry, hickory or any rough barked trees since they are noisy when brushed by hunting clothes. Also, you can usually eliminate beech as too solid a bark for contrast with your camo clothes. Extreme caution should be practiced if attempting to use screw-in steps on softwood trees such as aspen. The step could pull out with the weight of a hunter. The best trees are ash, maple, oak and walnut. Pine can also be an excellent choice if you are allowed to cut limbs for climbing and directional shooting lanes. Since they maintain their needles during the hunting season, pines will provide an excellent background cover.

Be advised that the pine sap, or pitch, is sticky and can make a mess on clothes and hands.

In the various areas where I hunt, more than 100 different stands have been selected and cleared as I patterned various deer. Each year, due to changing conditions, I will cut about a dozen new stands while abandoning several old ones. The forest is constantly changing, causing the deer to adapt and change with it, and the avid hunter soon follows.

You should scout trails, looking for good tree stand sites immediately after the hunting season since those active trails will probably be used again next hunting season. Carry a note pad in your jacket pocket and record where you intend to construct your new stand sites. Select new stands in early spring when you can see trees clearly. Cutting your shooting lanes in the spring will not spook deer, plus the cuts will be healed before the average nimrod begins scouting. When you cut off branches, use them as barricades to help keep the deer on the trail and channeled into your shooting lanes. I have used a subtle dead tree barricade to change the trail slightly thereby allowing the use of a tree that had a desirable size and shape but originally was not properly situated along the natural trail. Remember, deer will take the path of least resistance and will walk around brush through a clear opening.

Evening bow hunt

In the past couple of years, I have changed some of my hunting strategy in terms of the height of my stand above ground. In a tree stand located 12-15 feet high, I have been spotted by deer on a trail 20 yards away while drawing my bow and missed an opportunity for a shot. Now, when I set up in a sensitive place, like a bedding area or near oak trees, I will set my stand 25 to 30 feet above the ground. This requires the hunter to have a completely scent free approach but allows him to get a shot at deer entering from almost any direction.

Large trees with big limbs to help break your silhouette are best. On a breezy day, if you plan to use a tree stand, select one of your sites with few upper branches to minimize sway.

While preparing any new stand site, you must actually install the stand. Plus, if it has a seat, check your shooting lanes both sitting and standing. Incidentally, while standing, the bow extends higher than you might think and overhead clearance must be obtained. By the same token, extend your bow arm to be sure that when the bow is released, the bow limbs will not hit any branches. If the stand is for a gun hunt, a branch that will help hold your gun steady for a long shot could be mighty handy.

If you are locating your stand along a trail that curves, select a tree on the inside of the curve. Deer approaching from either direction will be looking ahead on the trail, scanning the outside of the curve.

I use a fruit tree trimming extension to cut off the high limbs that could interfere with my shot. Also, you will need to revisit all of your stand sites just prior to hunting season to prune any minor new growth. After trimming your shooting lanes, remove your stand and climbing steps and leave nothing behind. It usually takes me a couple of hours for each site.

It is a good practice never to use nails for your steps or your stand. In future years they could cause injuries to chain saw operators or if left in a lumber tree, the mill saw blade could be damaged.

If possible, design to set your stand on the west side of the tree for the morning hunt since you have better concealment in a shadow than in sunlight. Another consideration is to have the sun in the deer's eyes with the dark side of the tree hiding the hunter.

Locating the stand on the backside of a tree, opposite the trail, is a good idea in some instances. If only a small tree is available for a stand, or if the best tree is too close to the trail or where no other trees help break your silhouette such as in a tree line or sparsely wooded area, would be examples.

You practice shooting all year around, and you even have a full dress rehearsal in all of your hunting clothes, but do you ever practice putting your tree perch up? Do you go out at night, in cold weather or in the rain, wearing your heavy hunting gear, and climb 15 to 20 feet or higher up a tree with your steps and actually put your stand up? Probably not, but it would be a wise idea. One season when I had purchased a new portable stand and had shot many times from it, I discovered on opening day that my bow with arrows in the bow quiver would not fit into the bow holder.

Speaking of practice, shots from an elevated stand require experience. Most importantly, you must be sure to bend at the waist when shooting, to maintain the angle between your bow arm and body similar to the angle used to set your sight pins, or you will shoot high. A safety belt or harness is absolutely necessary for this type of leaning shot. If you practice from a high platform, such as your roof top, securely attach a safety belt prior to shooting. Move your target to every possible location including directly under your stand. I missed a nice eight-point while he stood directly under my stand with my feet about ten feet above his back. I waited too long to release as he approached and the arrow actually raised off the arrow rest when I leaned out and tried to shoot beneath me. Remember to practice shooting from the back of a tree, especially if some of your stands are intended to be set up on the backside. You also should recognize that a doe might take the trail to your front while the mossyhorn survivor tries to slip through behind your tree.

Use a safety belt around the tree while climbing to install the steps or stand. When you climb into your stand be certain that the first thing you do is to securely fasten your safety belt or harness. Make it a habit to do this prior to hauling up your equipment. Never climb into the stand while carrying your gun or bow. Tie a retrieve string onto your belt loop. When you are safely belted into your stand, haul up your equipment and stow the string in your pocket. Make sure that your safety belt allows you to sit or stand and keep it attached while in your stand. Some of us have even been known to take a short nap while hunting.

Some regulations prohibit a step from penetrating the tree more than 1/2", which, for a thick barked tree, would be unsafe to climb on. While hunting these areas, I switch to my climbing blocks. The blocks that I use are modeled after the one designed by the late Bill Wadsworth. Use a 4 1/2" long 2" x 4", with grooves routed in the face and the edges chiseled off. Stain or camo paint as desired all but the top of the step. The lighter color of the wood on top will be more visible in dim light climbing conditions. Drive several finishing nails into the top, leaving 1/8" extended to provide traction when slick. Finally, drill a hole through and attach a 10 foot long heavy nylon string or strap. If you are climbing a small diameter tree, simply run the string around the tree and then wrap, or frap it tightly around the block. For larger trees, use a double slip knot to secure the block to the tree. The slip knot will allow easy removal even after climbing on the block.

Tree stand accidents happen fast, and they happen to even the most experienced hunters. Since tree stand related accidents do occur, keep in mind that falls can kill. Broken legs, arms and spinal injuries can also be the result of a fall with the possibility of permanent paralysis. Every year I read about fatal accidents and injuries from tree stands in the states where I hunt. For your own survival, carry emergency equipment in your pocket, not in your pack, which might still be hanging on the stand if you should fall to the ground. As a minimum, include a whistle, flashlight and a first aid kit.

The single most important variable to consider when deciding which stand to use for a particular hunt is wind

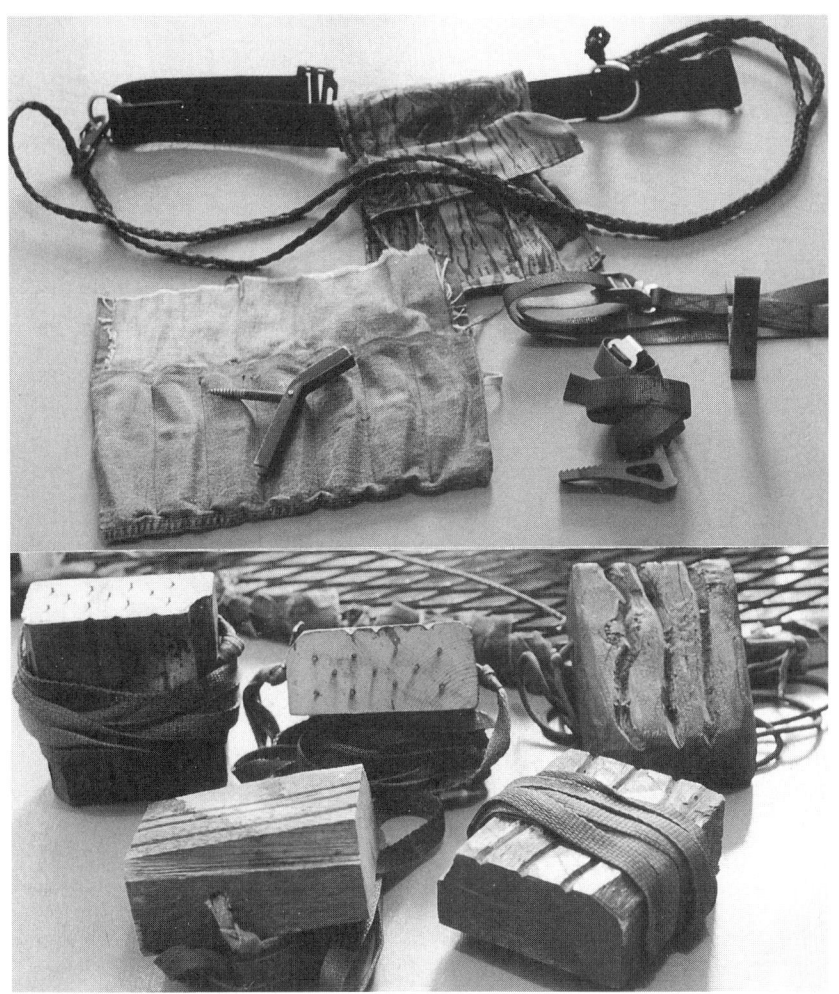

Top: Denim bag holds 7 screw-in steps while strap-on steps are carried in pouch on climbing belt. Bottom: Climbing blocks strap on quickly.

direction. On the day that you hunt, list all of your downwind stands and sort out which of those to hunt based on time of day, hunting pressure and deer activity. If you have a swirling downdraft breeze, do not waste your best stand site on this hunt. Some stands are better to save for the perfect conditions. If trail watching, it is best to approach your stand site from downwind since deer are expected to enter the shooting lane upwind. If you intend to rattle or lure a deer toward your tree, you should enter from upwind since the deer will normally check downwind prior to their final approach. For instance, if you plan to enter a stand near the feeding area for an evening bow hunt you should select

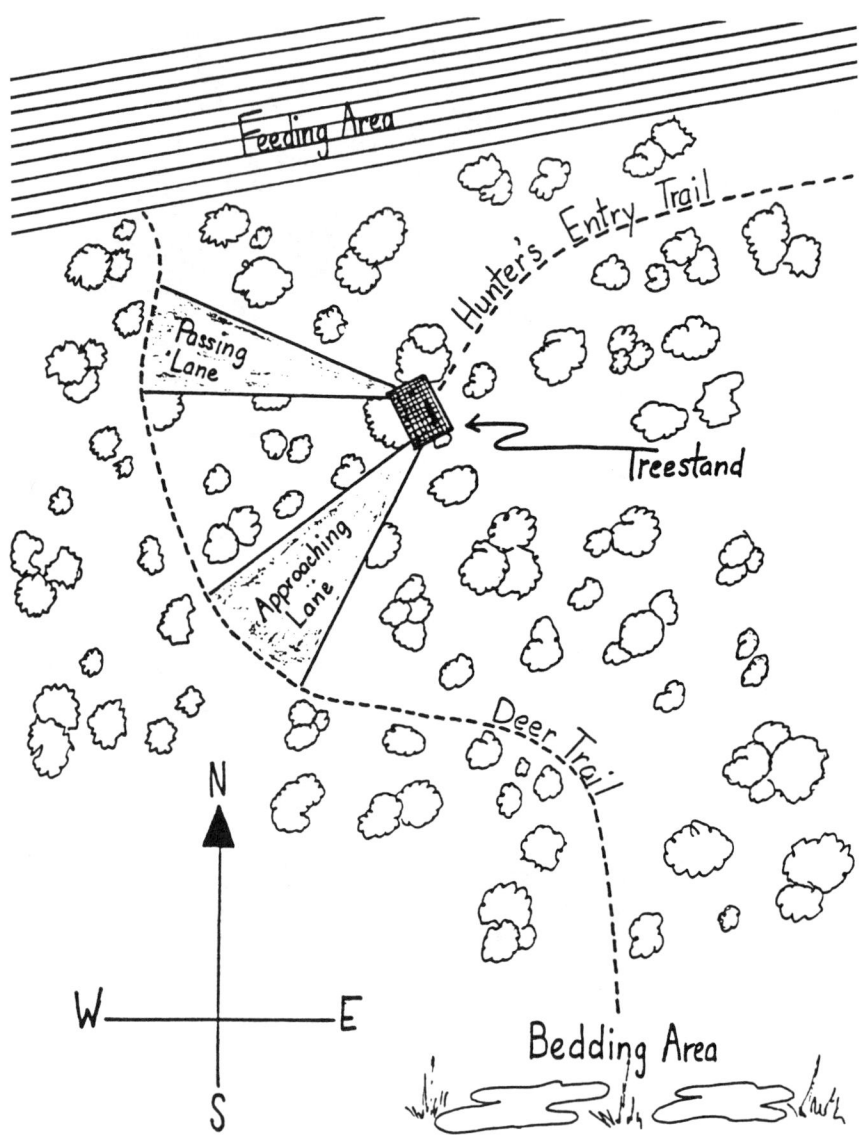

Evening hunt, South-West wind: Hunter enters thicket from downwind, sets stand on the back of a tree (East side), on the inside of the curve, about 50 yards from the clearing.

the east side of the tree for best shadow concealment. If the wind is west/southwest then you should select a tree on the east/northeast side of the trail and enter from the east, setting up on the backside of the tree. With your shooting lanes previously cut from the inside of the curve, you will have the best advantage for a shot into the vitals if you let the deer enter the passing lane, not the approaching shooting lane.

In addition to wind direction, stand sitters must also be aware of thermals. They carry your scent up and down instead of horizontally. The longer you occupy your stand, the greater the possibility of your warm scent mushrooming down around the tree and reaching the trail. When hunting, take a screw-in hook so that your gun, bow, fanny pack or possibles bag can be suspended, freeing your hands. Some bow hunters even remove their bow quiver while on stand.

One good hunting strategy is to drag scent into a shooting lane. Do this by dragging a lure in a loop about 100 yards out from your stand and back. If you have a large tree between your stand and the trail, place the scent container along the trail by the tree. Any deer that investigates, will have their head and eyes behind the tree while their body is exposed to the hunter, regardless of the direction of approach.

When preparing to climb out of your stand, be sure to lower your equipment and also to swing it out of the way. Do this while your safety belt is still attached. One evening, while hurrying out of my stand, I got careless and lost my footing a few steps from the ground and fell the last few feet onto my equipment. Luckily, I only ripped my pants, scraped my shin, chin and ego and severely bent two of my arrows at the fletching end.

If you leave your stand locked in the tree overnight and remove your screw-in steps, planning to return before daylight, leave small twigs protruding from the holes so you can locate them easily in the dark.

Successful tree stand hunters will be rewarded after hauling stand in by the enjoyable task of hauling buck out. Think safety at all times while tree stand hunting.

Always wear a saftey belt or harness in a tree stand! Attach some foliage to break up the straight lines of the stand.

*Tracks in a freshly fallen snow
will always lead to a deer.*

THE SECOND HUNT

What is considered by many to be the second hunt, involves the recovery of the deer after it has been shot by bullet or broadhead. I have helped trail both gunshot and bow shot deer for thousands of yards. Although it can be a time consuming effort, it is a true test of a hunter's trail reading skills and can be an exciting adventure.

The hunter begins gathering evidence immediately after the shot, relative to the point of the hit and the route of the escaping deer. The reaction of the deer to the hit is the first piece of information recorded by the hunter. Next, is the path of the wounded animal for as far as he can see or hear it. Finally, after the woods has quieted down, the hair in the vicinity of the hit, and the blood sign complete the basis for the trailing technique.

Before you move from the location where you shot at the deer, pinpoint the exact position of the deer, take a bearing, and estimate the distance of the shot. Mark the location where you are standing with surveyors tape and memorize the path taken by the escaping deer. Review the body action of the deer at the moment of your hit. Did the deer hump-up, indicating a body shot, or show any unusual posture that could indicate the location of the hit? A gut shot deer will sometimes kick out with their hind legs at the instant of impact. When it fled, was its tail down or was it running in a crouched position, both of which will usually confirm a solid hit? Did you notice any limping, staggering or irregular pattern to its normal bounding run? Did the deer awkwardly run into brush or trees in its attempt to escape? A heart shot deer will often make a startled jump when shot, followed by a head long burst into the brush. A friend ended up with a handful of tines after his heart shot eight-point smashed full tilt into an oak tree and broke both antlers during its death run.

How long you should wait before following the trail is still debated, even by experienced hunters. If your shot hit a vital organ, with the proper equipment, the deer will die quickly, often within 50 to 100 yards. Regardless of whether you are hunting with a gun or bow, give the animal time to settle down before making any move at all. The worst thing you can do is to alert the animal to the fact that it is being pursued.

Several circumstances may affect your decision on a proper waiting period. If the weather is cool, you certainly can afford to wait a little longer. Rain or snow may dictate that you get on the trail immediately so that you do not lose evidence. Night time sign reading is more difficult and will not allow a follow up shot if you should jump the wounded animal while trailing.

Normally, when several minutes have passed and the woods is back to normal, I will very quietly investigate the vicinity where the deer was standing when it was hit. If possible, include in your search, the exact route that your bullet or arrow took. Occasionally, a nick on a branch or tree will verify a deflection to the intended trajectory. Focus on finding the hairs cut when the bullet or broadhead entered the deer. Use these hairs to help identify the point of impact. Look for your arrow from a pass through shot if bow hunting and inspect the blood and particles on it. If gun hunting, try to determine if your bullet passed through by searching for blood on the far side of the trail. In either case, this information will be helpful in trailing the wounded deer. If blood is found on only one side of the trail, it will allow you to check the direction of the deer while trailing, and prohibit it from fooling you by backtracking.

Author holds lantern while Jim Fisher ties marker over blood trail.

If blood is found, study the color of the blood to help decide if a vital organ was hit. Review the blood and hair colors shown in the table. Long trailing adventures can often be avoided by allowing the animal adequate time to bed and expire. Do not hesitate to wait an hour before starting to trail a wounded animal. If blood is not found, or only a small amount is detected, do not try to rationalize that your shot was a miss or only a flesh wound and not worth a trailing effort. Follow the trail until you are positive that your shot was not a mortal wound. The blood flow often starts 30-50 yards from the shot location, flows heavily for a short distance, and then decreases to only a few drops after 100 to 150 yards. Also, the fat layer between the body cavity and the skin can clog the wound quickly so that very little blood will flow externally. One season, my brother shot at a nice 10-point with a 30-30 carbine, but the buck showing no indication of a hit, ran off with a doe. When the doe came past me on the other side of the woods, she was alone. After a half hour search along her approximate back trail, we found the trophy buck which had left no trailable blood, even though shot in the heart.

HIT ZONE	DEER REACTION	HAIR	BLOOD
Lungs	Runs hard, often on back trail. Drops within several hundred yards.	Medium length, brown to light brown.	Pink, frothy with bubbles.
Heart	Sudden jump, full run into everything. Dies quickly.	Brown.	Dark red.
Liver	Jumps and runs short distance. Drops soon if not pursued.	Light brown or long white.	Thick & dark.
Stomach or intestine	Hunched posture. Acts sick to stomach as it walks away. Will stop and bed if not pursued.	Short white or short lt brown.	Little blood, but greenish yellow slime containing food particles.
Back	If spine hit, then paralysis, if not, then runs easily away.	Long, dark brown with black tips.	Very little blood, unless artery, then dark red.

If you determine that your shot has hit the stomach or intestines of the deer, this presents a different problem. Undoubtedly, the deer will die, but it will take time and may be very difficult to trail. If pursued, it can run a long way before dying. Your best approach is to leave the area for about 6 hours which should allow the deer time to lie down and die.

As a deer hunter, you have a legal and moral obligation to stay on the trail and find your deer. To be successful in recovering the deer, you must abandon the hunt and concentrate on reading trail sign. Closely examine tracks of the wounded animal to note any peculiarities that might enable you to sort out tracks if mixed with other deer. It is best to trail with two or three people, keeping the trail between you and moving quietly and slowly as though you were stillhunting. With two people trailing, one should wait by the last blood found while the other methodically scouts ahead for further sign. Both should use hand signals and refrain from talking as they trail. Mark the blood trail by tying surveyors tape or tissue paper on overhanging limbs or tall weeds. This will enable you to establish a general direction of the deer's escape route. Remove all trail markers when the game is found or the trail is lost. Be sure to look on row crops, grasses, bushes, rocks or tree trunks when you cannot find blood on the bare ground or autumn leaves. When trailing, note the highest location of blood on bushes to help verify the point of the hit. If it has rained, the underside of leaves may still retain some fresh blood and you will need to turn them over to find it. Dried blood is difficult to spot since it blends in with the fall foliage. Blood splatters in the direction of a well hit, fast moving deer, like the fingers on your hand.

If you lose the trail, use common sense and your knowledge of the area to continue the search. Most of the time, a mortally wounded deer will instinctively head for the safety of thick security cover. Quite often this route will be downhill to the heavy growth along a stream or swamp. Use the blood trail to project the probable direction and then thoroughly search likely areas for a few hundred yards ahead. Keep alert for the wounded animal to rise from its bed so that a follow up shot can be made. Investigate anything white which could be the belly of the downed deer. Look carefully under brush piles or fallen trees. Check any concentrated activity of crows, magpies or buzzards which might indicate that they have found your dead deer. At night, a white gas lantern helps illuminate the entire area, making sign reading easier. Fresh blood shows up brightly in this type of light and it works much better than a flashlight for trailing.

Generally, if a deer looses 35% of its blood volume, it will die. This includes internal as well as external bleeding. A whitetail deer has roughly 1 ounce of blood for every pound that it weighs. Therefore, a 160 pound deer has about 160 ounces of blood and will lose about 56 ounces or about 3 1/2 pints before dying.

Take your best shot, assume a hit, and then review all of the evidence before beginning the second hunt for your deer. There is no way to describe the feeling of satisfaction accompanying the moment that you reach the successful end of a difficult trail where your trophy is waiting.

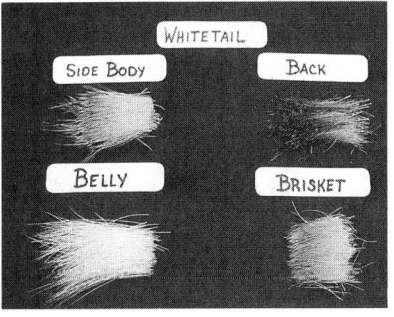

Whitetail body hair: Side body is medium length brown to light brown; back is long coarse, dark brown with black tips; belly is medium to long white and fine; brisket is short, light brown and twisted at base of neck.

Teaching axiom:
I tell you = you forget
I show you = you remember
I let you do = you understand

WANTED: A FEW GOOD HUNTERS

As hunters, we need an awakening. We participate in a sport that is no longer simply accepted as the normal pursuit of survival. A passive position is likened to a fence sitter and you will soon find yourself with a sore crotch and no hunting privileges. If you are a hunter, it means that you use a gun or a bow in the pursuit of wild game. Responsible means that we are each liable and accountable for our own conduct and actions. To become a responsible hunter, a person must not only be knowledgeable of game laws or regulations but must also obey them. In addition, the hunter must follow the unwritten laws of conduct and sportsmanship. Hunting is not a right that is guaranteed to everyone regardless of his/her actions, it is a privilege that can be revoked. The true measure of an ethical, responsible hunter is evidenced by ones own behavior. If you are a true hunter, you will be responsible to yourself, other hunters, the resource, landowners, other people, children and domestic animals used in hunting. Each of these categories of responsibility has specific considerations, some of which are listed in the following paragraphs.

When you are by *yourself* in the woods, your actions reflect your true worth, in other words, your heart. As stated, knowing the game laws is not enough—you must also obey them. Laws are made to provide equal opportunity for all to hunt while managing the game. You must be trustworthy in all of your actions. The unwritten laws of sportsmanship require personal judgment. It would be unsportsmanlike to kill all the quail in a covey, to shoot a buck with his antlers enmeshed with another buck in combat, or to claim another hunter's deer when you see it fall nearby. Do not succumb to peer pressure that may cause you to take shots that you

Poachers are criminals, not sportsmen, and they are stealing your deer. Photo by Richard Fields, I.D.N.R.

should not, or worse yet, to fantasize so that you visualize a deer that is not actually there. It could trick you into an accidental shooting of a person. In your personal effort to promote the sport of hunting, you should attend and encourage others to become involved in hunter education classes, first as a student, and maybe later as an instructor. You should join organizations and clubs and support their goals. It is important to patronize the manufacturers, advertisers, newspapers and magazines that back our sport. It is also necessary to advise the sponsors of anti-hunting propaganda of your displeasure.

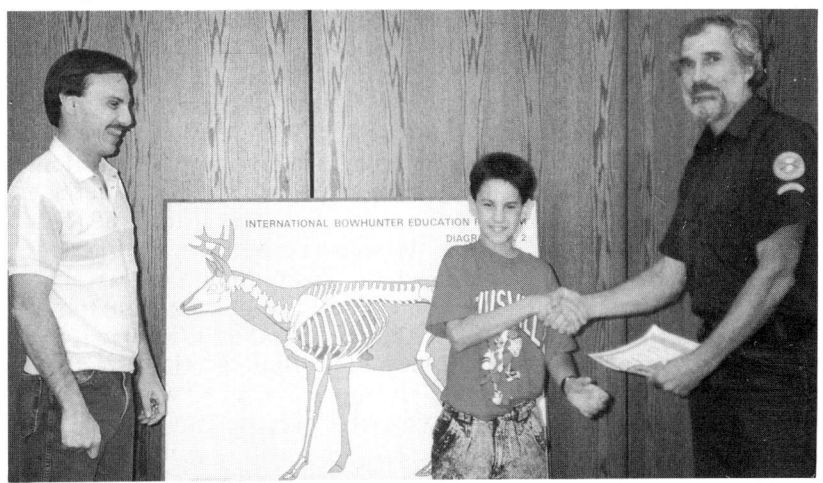

Michael Hutton receives Hunter Education Certification from Instructor Nobel while his father Fred, who also took the course, approves. If you hunt "with" your children, you will not have to hunt "for" your children.

While hunting, remember that there are usually *other hunters* in the woods. They may not be hunting the same critters as you, but if they are, they may choose a different method than you have. Do not criticize or rebuke their selection of equipment. For example: Respect their choice of a shotgun for deer hunting while you prefer a muzzleloader. They may prefer a scoped sight, you may not. Another hunter may select a recurve bow but you decide that a compound is best for you. If you are participating in a hunt with others, know their location, be aware of any pertinent medical history of each, and volunteer to help them track, locate or remove game from the woods. If someone that you are hunting with practices illegal hunting or unsafe gun handling, warn them, and then discontinue your association with them unless they correct their actions. Have knowledge of the area where you hunt. Always carry a compass and survival gear so that other hunters are not called upon to spend their time rescuing you. Comply with sportsmen's unwritten laws such as "the law of first blood" for bow hunters. This law implies that the kill belongs to the first bowhunter who shot his arrow into a vital organ and is able to trail the game. We have a responsibility to other hunters to inform them of the importance of joining a club or organization to support the sport that they love, before their attitude of apathy loses this opportunity for all of us. With other hunters, the most important consideration is to be absolutely positive of your identification of the game before you shoot. Remember, once you shoot, you can never take the shot back.

The *resource*, considered by many to be the most important ingredient of responsibility, includes both wildlife and the environment. As a result of conservation efforts by sportsmen, the national whitetail population, which reached a dangerously low level of 500,000 a few years ago, is now about 14 million. It was originally the American sportsmen that called for federal and state wildlife conservation programs, for parks and refuges to conserve wildlife, and for laws to stop the dangerous practice of market hunting. This information is from the "Protect What's Right" pamphlet produced by The Wildlife Conservation Fund of America for the Wildlife Legislative Fund of America. As a hunter, you should strive for a sure clean kill to minimize trauma of the animal and to eliminate the possibility of wounding and perhaps losing the quarry. If you are successful in your hunt, take photographs worthy of your trophy and mount them in an album. Thorough knowledge of the location of the vital organs in all game that you hunt is basic. Immediately upon retrieving your kill, you should protect the meat. Keep it free from dirt and moisture while cooling it and protecting it from flies and other insects. Marksmanship, proper equipment and staying within your personal limits will make you a more responsible hunter. Your equipment should be kept in perfect condition, properly prepared for hunting, and properly cleaned and stored after the season. By law, every reasonable effort must be made to retrieve game that is killed or wounded. One of the main criticisms of the anti-hunter is that hunters do not always eat what they kill. If you have extra meat, share it, but never waste it. Many organizations now have programs in affect that will distribute your extra venison to needy people. Some hunters, that own land, plant food plots or cover crops to help game survive. Plant a crop with nutrition, that deer like, and one that will ripen when local crops are harvested. A feed with high protein and calcium, such as Ladino clovers, is an excellent selection, while a crop with a high percentage of phosphorus seems to enhance antler growth the most. The environment also needs our protection, so be sure to clean up your camp, extinguish your campfire and pick up everything including the cartridges from your target shooting.

Habitat, which is dwindling, is a critical ingredient for conservation, so do whatever you can to minimize this loss.

Leave fur bearing animals alone! Photo by Eric Nobel

The law requires that you obtain permission to hunt from the *landowner*. Keep in mind that when he gives you permission, you are a guest on his property. Fewer landowners, all the time, are willing to let strangers hunt on their property. When you do receive permission, written, if possible, be sure to have a clear understanding about the limits. This includes the area to hunt, time of day or season, whether you can shoot a buck, doe or either, if it is allowable to bring a friend, and simple things, like where you can park your vehicle. Be sure that you let the landowner know when you expect to enter his land and also when you leave. Cross the fence only at a post and be sure not to cross onto a neighbors land without receiving prior permission. Offer the landowner some of the daily harvest, or better yet, some of the processed meat. Remember them at Christmas with a card and a note of thanks. Do not hesitate to surprise them with a useful personal gift, but never make it alcohol. A hunter orange safety vest for the owner to wear around the farm during hunting season makes a thoughtful gift. The best gift might be some of your time to help them with their chores. If land is posted "No Hunting", it means just what it says. Even if you are blood trailing a wounded animal, it is unlawful to trespass on private property. In this case, a law enforcement officer might be able to assist by getting you special permission to enter the property solely for the purpose of retrieving the trailed animal.

Whether you are in the field or not, you must learn to respect the rights of *other people*. They have a right in the woods to hike, enjoy nature, take photographs, dig ginseng or whatever they are pursuing. Proper disposition of entrails, following field dressing, especially where non-hunters might coexist in the woods, should be practiced. Proper game bags or covering of animals while transporting is very important to the public image of hunters. Do not bother to debate with anti-hunters. Ask yourself, "Could someone ever convince me not to hunt?" No! Absolutely not! Antis feel the same way. When it comes to anti-hunters, some policies concerning interaction should be predetermined. Presently 48 states have hunter harassment laws that provide for the prosecution of persons intentionally disrupting your hunt. Foremost, keep your poise. Keep in mind that the interference is short term and not directed personally at you, but at hunters in general, and your behavior represents all other hunters in North America. Observe gun safety rules and never make any threatening gestures that could later be used against you in court. Record every detail of their activities, including descriptions of the perpetrators, license plates, etc., after verifying their intentional harassment of your hunt. If you are involved in a classroom confrontation, advise the anti's that no political statements are allowed and ask them to leave since they are disrupting the class. If they refuse, call the authorities to have them removed. Take the opportunity to explain the conservation role and other attributes of the hunter to the remaining approximately 75% of the voting population, or about 160,000,000 adults which are non-hunters, but voters. Explain the reason for the increase in game due to sportsmen, management agencies and our contributions as a result of the taxes collected from the Pittman-Robertson Act of 1937 which provides an 11% tax on all guns, bows, bullets and sporting equipment. Last year, appropriations from this source were more than $150 million bringing the total funds to over $2.4 billion, for state game and fish wildlife agencies, since its enactment. The nearly 16 million licensed hunters annually contribute over $430 million from license sales. Since 1923 the sales of state hunting licenses, tags and permits have provided more than $6 billion toward wildlife management (including non-game), habitat acquisition and enhancement, plus conservation law enforcement, shooting range construction and Hunter Education. This information

Ruth Nobel (author's mother) enjoys picking woods flowers.

from the Hunter Services Division of the National Rifle Association also reflects that 360,000 jobs throughout the nation are dependent upon hunting related expenditures. Remember, Wildlife Conservation receives about $600 million annually from sport hunter's revenues.

The future of our sport may well be in the hands of *children*. Today's youth may be a small percentage of our population, but they are 100% of our future. We must be sure that proper attention and education are provided for our youth. We should expose all interested children to the opportunity

Eric Nobel (author's son) explains to his son Barret "Bear" about the responsibilities of gun or bow handling and hunting.

to hunt. In many states, the youth license allows hunting at a very reasonable cost. We should encourage our youth to attend hunter education classes, special hunting seminars or shows and to become members of hunting clubs. We must make an extra effort to pass on the attitude and skill of a true sportsman. This includes taking your child or the child of a friend hunting with you. Teach them about firearm safety and make time in your schedule for target practice with the youngsters. Instead of discarding your sporting magazines, pass them on to a receptive school teacher to use in class, or give them to interested children in your neighborhood.

Take proper care of domestic animals.

Some *domestic animals* are used in hunting. In the western states, horses, mules and llama are used for transportation and/or pack animals. However, dogs are the most widely used hunting animal. Be sure that you provide proper exercise, food and care for these animals within your control. Even the dogs on the Iditarod dog race have foot protection from ice crystals.

Remember the future. Set your goals to become an ethical, responsible hunter and encourage all others that you are associated with to follow your example. Never mix alcohol or drug use with any hunting or target shooting activity. Report any game law violations to the proper authorities to help stop poaching. Pursue these responsible efforts and you will have many enjoyable hunting seasons, plus a hunting heritage to pass on to your children and grandchildren.

The Christophers, of Sawyer, Michigan, have a right to enjoy a family hike in the woods.

I only hunt on days that end with a "y"

Author packing in for a bow hunt with Don Kubasch.

ENJOYING THE HUNT

Ran across an old timer sitting on a stump while I was hunting the other day and asked him, "Having any luck?"

He happily answered, "Yes, lots of luck!"

I looked around to see what he had shot so far but didn't see any game, so I said, "I don't see anything that you shot."

Smiling back, he answered, "I haven't shot anything. I haven't even seen or heard anything. I'm having fun, and I feel just plain lucky to be able to be out here in the woods."

"Bucky" gets a nice doe!

He is fortunate to enjoy his outing, to be able to enjoy his time in the woods. Too much pressure is put on hunters to succeed, when success is measured only with a kill and harvest of game.

Next time ask a hunter: "Did you have fun and enjoy your time in the woods today?"

If these deer knew what I was thinking they would not be sniffing around my hat.

"You can hardly notice any damage from out here!"

My greatest regret is that I have but one lifetime to hunt whitetail deer.

IS YOUR PHOTOGRAPH WORTHY OF YOUR TROPHY?

Looking back a few years I recognize an irreversible mistake that I have made on several occasions. Regrettably, my trophies of small game, birds and big game are not well represented in pictures. Typically, photographs are incidental to the hunt, almost a bashful admission of vanity, and very little posing time is allowed. Many hunters pretend that they do not really care if they photograph their trophy or not. Nothing could be further from the truth. The game you kill is exciting for you at that moment and worthy of future viewing to re-live those happy moments for yourself or to share them with others. Good photos will enable you to accomplish this while poor efforts could be more of an embarrassment. This chapter will present ideas, even if they seem obvious, plus provide some tips to help each hunter record the moment.

First of all, take your camera and adequate film into the field so you can capture "on location" drama. The actual setting for game is usually the best memory. Protect your equipment with a hard case plus a plastic bag to keep moisture out. The telephoto lens is not needed. However, unless your camera has it built in, take the flash attachment. Not only do many hunts end in dim light conditions, but in the woods, especially under a hat brim, extra light helps illuminate the hunter and his subject.

Pack your camera so that you can take on-site photos prior to field dressing.

For processing and printing a 4x6 color print, it costs about 41¢ each including the film. Slides are less expensive for processing but the film costs more so each slide will be about 48¢. The slide is necessary if your audience is large, but for a photo album or just to show to your friends, photographs are cheaper and also less expensive for an enlargement of that special shot. A 5x7 enlargement might cost $1.50 while an 8x10 can be made for about $3.00.

Recyclable cameras, about the size of a rangefinder, are now available with several options. You can select wide angle, telephoto or flash with your camera, and after taking your photographs, simply mail the entire camera back to the manufacturer. The total cost of these prints will average 75 cents each, but you do not risk your camera on the pack trip.

Pictures should be carefully posed, with structures, vehicles, or other distractions removed from the background. Also, be sure to keep the photographers shadow off the subject and out of the picture. Never allow beverage containers or other litter to ruin your photograph.

Author with 8-point whitetail.

To obtain sharp images, focus on the subject and squeeze off camera shots as though you were shooting your rifle. If unsure of light conditions, bracket the recommended setting with a more open and a more closed aperture. It might waste a few photos but you may never get the opportunity to duplicate the situation.

Bright colors, such as hunter orange, can offset the natural woods surroundings, providing an exciting contrast. Never allow raw meat or blood to be the bright color in your trophy shots. Cover the wound with a leaf or turn the animal around to eliminate these damaged areas. If the camera is taken into the field, some excellent photos can be taken prior to field dressing. If the tongue is hanging out, simply cut it off. Smooth the hair (or feathers) of your game for best appearance. Spend a moment preparing the trophy for its final photograph.

A dab of vaseline or water on deer eyes will give them a lifelike shine plus holding their ears forward while photographing makes them look alive. In contrast, most pictures of buck antelope have their ears held down to create the appearance of longer horns. Be sure both antlers are clearly visible and do not let them blend into the background, thereby losing some of their detail. When people view your buck pictures, it seems they always like to count the points.

Remember to take several photos with the animal dominating the picture. For example, place deer in the foreground with hunter behind, similar to holding your fish toward the camera at arms length. A good photo that provides an excellent example, poses the hunter approaching the down animal from behind. The hunter can even be in view, but out of focus for a special effect. Get your hunting partners into a few of the pictures to record the companionship.

Author with 4X5 mule deer, Montrose, Colorado.

If bowhunting, capture a photo with the hunter crouching beside the animal showing bow limb displaying manufacturers name for a point of interest. Also, for a different but effective record of the hunt, place the bow or firearm across the animal without the hunter. This may be necessary if you hunt alone and do not have a timer on your camera.

If you are unable to take actual field photos, pose when you obtain a camera. Arrange game on the ground simulating the hunting environment and dress with the same garments worn

Hunter approaching downed deer.

Take a photo of deer/equipment without the hunter.

while hunting. If you simply slip on your hunting coat, invariably the photo will reveal your white tennis shoes making the whole setup look phony. Your trophy deserves better and the hunter has a responsibility to the animal. Be creative, take plenty of shots with different poses from various distances, angles and heights.

Some hunting magazines publish members photos when they meet certain criteria. Use the following guidelines for keepsake photos in your hunting album. Keep in mind, they will probably be viewed by hunters and nonhunters, both young and old.

As a minimum, your trophy photograph should:
1) Have little or no blood showing.
2) Be in focus and properly exposed.
3) Not have the animal's tongue visible.
4) Have the trophy tastefully positioned, not hanging by a rope or in a truck bed.
5) Provide a natural setting with no structure or vehicle in the background.
6) Never have litter or beverage container (especially alcoholic) shown.
7) Remove your sunglasses and strike a happy pose.

Pose with mounted deer in a natural setting.

"Wilderness areas can not be re-created by hindsight."
Aldo Leopold

WILDERNESS VISIONS

Wilderness visionaries such as Bob Marshall, Aldo Leopold, John Muir, Siguard F. Olson and others were wise enough and concerned enough to follow their foresight, pursue the politicians and convince them to set aside wilderness areas for future generations to enjoy. President "Teddy" Roosevelt, our greatest hunting president, helped greatly in this effort.

There are certain places we see while exploring these wilderness areas that we never forget. We do not consciously look for these regions of perfect solitude and beauty while hunting, but occasionally we find them. In retrospect, it seems that I have discovered only one per decade as an average. Even dedicated hunters will momentarily forget the hunt as they stop and record the landscape with an indelible cerebral image. The view is generally too large to be photographed adequately. These spots of everlasting beauty fill a space in our minds. The dates do not matter since the image never fades. When you encounter these wilderness visions, you will know and you will remember. Perhaps the weather, time of day or season, or even your emotional mood play a part in the value of these visions.

Sandstone formations in Northeast Ohio.

I remember the first vision while still in high school whitetail hunting along the edge of a glacial moraine in northern Ohio. I was spellbound by the 100 foot high vertical sedimentary stone walls rising abruptly from the wetlands. Crevices in the rock formed caves that stretched hundreds of feet under ground, some containing ice year round. This unnatural looking wall of stone was an exciting view that I shall never forget.

A few years later, with the Pacific Ocean breaking close behind me, I topped a ridge on Kodiak Island, Alaska searching for the Sitka blacktail deer. What I found was a panoramic view some 3000 to 4000 yards across a natural amphitheater gouged out of stone. I sat on a flat rock with my feet in lichens and gazed across the gray-green mountain floor strewn with boulders the size of trucks. I forgot about deer as I wondered how many people would get the opportunity to view such an enormous and magnificent sight.

Aerial view of wilderness area in Alaska.

The Rocky Mountains offer many spectacular views but two stand out memorably for me. The first was during a morning hunt on Gem Mountain in the Lolo National Forest of western Montana. As I dropped over the rim onto the north slope, I entered a gentle valley, where the tall Ponderosa Pines formed a canopy shielding the sun. The ground for hundreds of yards was covered with spring fed bear grass. The wind, dodging its way between the tree trunks and shadows of the pines, constantly changed the color of the grass as it moved. It was one of the most beautiful and peaceful sights of the mountains.

Several years later and several hundred miles southeast, near Pikes Peak, Colorado, I was again halted by the beauty of the Rockies. Hunting out of Cripple Creek, with Pikes Peak as a referee, we pushed through a wilderness area searching ahead for elk. The incline that I was following suddenly broke into a plateau along the slope. This slightly concave, mostly level area trapped moisture and invited game. It was like a park, a

The Pintlers Wilderness Area in the Rocky Mountains.

nourishing oasis among the pines, surrounded by rocky slopes, almost barren of vegetation.

The latest beauty of nature that captured my imagination occurred while turkey hunting in the Hoosier National Forest, in Jackson County, Indiana. It was a small valley, compared to western scale, but it was favored by two streams and rich moist forest soil. The streams had each cut 30 foot deep runways down to bedrock. The sunlight filtered through the tall oak trees, made taller by their ridge top positions. These occasional rays highlighted the young ferns and the old mossy covered logs of fallen giants from the original forest. Dark slate rock outcroppings guarded the stream beds as they urged the many rough round geodes slowly along. It was a place of everlasting beauty.

As you hunt the wilderness areas, cherish these visions of unspoiled natural beauty. Allow yourself the time to enjoy them while you hunt. It is these precious moments which create the memories that will be yours forever.

As hunters grow older, their bodies get shorter while their stories get longer.

"Here's looking at you bud."
Photo by Ted Rose

DEER CAMP SOCIETY

It is difficult to describe the excitement of anticipation preceding the annual deer camp. The planning of the hunt, lists of gear, readying of equipment, menus and estimation of groceries all become enjoyable tasks and occupy several months prior to the actual camp.

It is a gathering unlike any other. Hunters are brought together for meat, recreation and friendships. United with a common interest, deer hunters create a special bond of comradary. Like their predecessors, the mountain men and pioneers, they are mostly very independent, competitive personalities that form a fraternity in the deer camp society.

Whether deer camp consists of two hunters or a group, special friendships are formed or cemented. It does not matter if the hunting home is a cabin, a tent, the back of a pickup truck or the comforts of a travel trailer. Memorable experiences and great stories accompany the annual hunt and several of these are retold as a ritual each year.

Eric Reske and Lee Christopher boast several deer hanging in barn at Michigan camp.

Deer hunting stories are told by the veterans who kill their deer every year, while the newer hunters eagerly listen, hoping to learn their secrets. Strange or unusual tales are best remembered. There is always the story about one of the hunters that got severe gas pains while hunting and just barely got his britches down in time. Unfortunately for him, after he covered the ground, he took a step forward only to find that he had been standing on a leafy sapling that sprang back up and splattered his backside brown.

One of my favorite camp stories goes back a few years. In the good old days when we had plenty of energy, we deer hunted all day, or until we got our buck. Our simple tree stands consisted of a board about 18" long and 10" wide with the ends notched to fit into the crotch of a tree. There being no room for our lunch we would cache it at the base of the tree and cover it with leaves so the deer wouldn't see it and get spooked. To save time and eliminate noise, a small string would be attached to the lunch sack so that when the hunter got hungry, he could simply retrieve his bag.

One morning, a hunter not familiar to our camp, happened to sit at the base of my partner's tree. My friend, not wanting to cause a commotion, just let the other fellow sit there for a while. The longer he stayed, the more concerned my friend became that he would discover the lunch bag hidden under the leaves. Unable to wait any longer, my worried friend started to slowly pull on his string. At every rustle and twist of the lunch bag, the hunter at the base of the tree became alerted to something moving close by him. Finally, when the bag emerged from its leafy concealment and materialized dangling in front of the sitting intruder, he instinctively reached for it. My friend saw the peril that his precious lunch was in, and jerked it up a few feet, whereupon the uninvited hunter jumped to his feet and made a final desperate leaping grab for the flying bag. Frantically, my friend gathered another handful of string, pulling the cargo out of reach. At that moment the ground sitter finally looked up into the tree, and as his eyes met the downward glare of my friend, he uttered a choking groan as a realization of the phenomenon of the flying lunch bag became clear. Without a word, the embarrassed visitor left in a hurried exit down the trail.

The "hanging branch" was used for several years by Don Silvey and author.

Deer camps perpetuate, with hunters' offspring, relatives and even grandchildren eventually helping eternalize the annual event. Once a camp has been started, all participants should strive to reinforce this experience of fun, learning, adventure and harvest. After only a few days in camp with no shaving, little washing and roughing it, a man reverts back to his primitive ancestral ways, but this is all a part of the camp spirit.

The use of alcohol in camp can be permitted, or condoned,

"The Meat Hunters"
Lee Tracy—Montana,
Eric Reske—Indiana and
Bert Miller—Washington.

as a toast or social indulgence with responsible behavior, but only when the hunting equipment is stowed for the day. Drinking and hunting should never be mixed.

The tantalizing aroma of food cooking is often mixed with the wood smoke of camp while special culinary concoctions reserved for this occasion are prepared by the hunters. Where else can you find a 20 quart pot filled with chunks of cooked venison mixed with potatoes, onions, carrots, and tomatoes (real hunters don't eat celery) and kept hot all afternoon or until empty. You will soon notice that most recipes only require a single cooking container, since dishpan diarrhea is a common malady in camp. Some food always seems to taste better in hunting camp. Most hunters will agree that liver never tastes as good anywhere else. Ravenous appetites always see to it that no leftovers need to be stored for another warming. Good food and plenty of it is the reason that very few of us can lose weight at these fall rendezvous.

"Roughing It" in camp trailer are Dod, Don Kubasch, Mary Jane Nobel and Mike Musegades. Photo by Jan Kubasch

Stoking the campfire for the hungry hunters.

Deer camps are a hunting tradition with plenty of history. If you have not participated, I can only assure you that deer camps are as necessary as they are special, and it would not be a complete hunting season without them. Once you join the deer camp society, you will comprehend its value.

A hunting companion is a friend who is as happy to see you bag a deer as you would be to see him get one.

This buck fawn has dark hair swirls between his eyes and ears indicating the pedicels where antlers will form. Photo furnished by Richard English

THAT'S MY DEER!

It was about 4:30 AM when the hunters gathered in the large gymnasium to receive their hunt instructions and safety briefing from the military base commander. One especially excited pair of hunters was a father who was taking his 13-year-old son on the youth's first deer hunt. Leaving their vehicle in the predawn hours, the father instructed his son to return to the truck by noon if they should get separated while hunting.

About mid-morning, the youngster shot and killed a nice doe, his very first deer. Using the training that he had received in hunter education class, he field dressed the deer by himself, and attached his correctly notched temporary tag to the doe's leg. Since the deer was too heavy for him to drag, he left it and went out to the truck for help. When he and his father returned to retrieve the deer a short time later, they discovered that another hunter had come across the deer, cut off the boy's tag and stolen it. The father was irate as the two followed the drag trail to the road where the deer had been loaded into the thief's vehicle and was long gone. The father consoled the son for his loss but the young hunter did not give up. He knew that all deer had to be checked and the permanent metal tag attached prior to leaving the base. Although the father felt that it was a waste of time and that a positive identification of his son's doe was impossible, he agreed to try.

The vehicles of the successful hunters were already lined up at the check station where state biologists were recording the sex, weight, age and condition of every deer while tagging them.

The boy carefully inspected every doe in line and finally stopped in front of one and claimed, "That's my deer!" The adult with his tag on the deer sarcastically retorted, "I shot that doe, my tag is on it, and there is no way you could ever prove that it was yours."

The young hunter reached into his pocket and pulled out a small pink wedge shaped object. Opening the doe's mouth, he matched it exactly back into the doe's tongue where he had notched it before leaving the woods. The boy got his deer back and the "wannabe hunter" got the scorn that he deserved.

Young deer in overcrowded state park, with very little understory, barely survived the winter.

Nobody ever plans to take the last sip of water from his/her canteen.

PREPARE TO SURVIVE

None of us plan to get lost while hunting. Some of us will not even admit that we have ever been lost. It reminds me of the old mountain man statement, "I've never been lost, but I've been a mite confused for a few months."

When you are accustomed to hunting wood lots and small land parcels, it can be overwhelming to enter a national forest, especially in the western states, where the nearest road, perhaps a gravel one lane, might be 20 miles away in mountainous terrain. Whether you are entering a wilderness area or a local woods, each hunter has the individual responsibility to survive. Take this responsibility seriously and be fully prepared to save your own life. You can prepare yourself by conditioning your body and mind while readying your equipment. Prior to the day's hunt, let a reliable person know your plans and alternate plans. Upon returning from the hunt, contact your friend to let him know you are back. Report on the day's experiences and thank him for letting you use him in case an emergency developed.

Many years ago, while hunting an unfamiliar national forest with friends, I entered the woods during early morning darkness. About noon I decided to head back to camp for lunch. After walking for about an hour, I realized that I was lost and resorted to my compass. Foolishly, I had not taken bearings at camp, so I could only guess the correct direction. I guessed poorly and spent the afternoon, using my compass to maintain a straight line, walking out to the road. When I finally reached the road, I was about six long miles from camp and walked that distance, arriving just at dark. Everyone was proud of me and admired my dedication for hunting all day without breaking for lunch. They told me about the friendly .22 target competition that they had held together. I remembered hearing the shooting when I was lost but thought that our camp was in another direction and so I had walked the other way in my search. I never admitted this error to my friends.

In my opinion, walking and hiking are the best basic conditioning exercises, combined with some fast pace activity at least three times per week. Sports doctors describe a formula for a fast pulse rate which should be reached for a 20 minute period several times per week. You should increase your pulse to 70% of the resultant of 220 minus your age. Therefore, if you are 50 years old, you should exercise to a pulse rate of 119 beats per minute (220-50=170, 170x.70=119). It is equally important to precede this fast pace exercise with stretching and slow activity warm up exercises of several minutes each, and follow your heavy work out with a slow down, or cool down period, of mild activity for another five minutes. Stretching of your muscles is important to minimize cramping and promote flexibility. When you stretch, do not make it a painful, tissue ripping endurance contest, but, for best results, stretch with a steady 30 to 40 second taut hold, without bouncing. It should tell you something when the biggest complaint from hunting guides is the poor physical condition of their hunters. They arrive in camp without proper conditioning and cannot meet the vigors of the hunt and therefore do not give their best effort. Equally as important as conditioning your muscles is the toughening of your feet. If you rub blisters or otherwise create sore feet, you cannot effectively hunt on foot. You may be prepared mentally but not physically.

Preparing the mind includes the degree of readiness of intangibles such as spirit, attitude and the control of one's emotions. Hunting maturity allows you to enjoy the sport without peer pressure or social pressure. It enables the hunter to maintain control of his emotions, especially at the moment of excitement immediately preceding the shot, so that you do not let "buck fever" overcome your abilities. It keeps you from panicking in the face of danger or the knowledge that you are indeed lost and alone.

Attitude is not just important for good hunting concentration, but also for strength and endurance. With the proper positive attitude, a hunter can endure cold, hunger and other hardships to call on reserve energies for survival.

With knowledge comes confidence and this enhances your degree of hunting success along with your ability to survive.

When entering a new area or for a more thorough analysis of a familiar hunting area, the study of a map is recommended. Aerial maps can be obtained from A.S.C.S. or county survey offices, landowner names are listed in plat books sold at the county court house but topographic maps purchased from the state or a U.S.G.S. office may provide your best information.

Why should a hunter use a map? The first reason is for survival, while the second is to locate likely hunting sites. The top of the map will be north. After checking the scale of the map, so that you can estimate distances, check the declination. This is the difference, in degrees, between true or geographic north (GN) and your compass reading or magnetic north (MN). Your compass needle will point toward magnetic north so you will need to correct to true north for accurate map reading. If your area has a west declination, the amount should be added to the compass reading, while east declination is subtracted to obtain true north. Some of the areas where I hunt have a 20° declination and a correction is necessary for map coordination. Good advice is to borrow a page from the Indians' book of woodlore, and measure distance in terms of time, not miles traveled. To further simplify your hunt, forget magnetic declination, and stick to compass readings, recognizing that your route may not coordinate exactly with the map.

Pattern your study of the map to learn the features of the area. Most importantly, locate the road system surrounding your hunting area, and then determine the land boundaries where you have permission to hunt. Next, lay out the drainage areas, paying particular attention to ditches, streams, rivers, their direction, and any road crossings. Finally, look for features including man made and natural geographic ones. Memorize the location of high hills, steep slopes, fields, swamps, RR tracks, pipelines, power lines, etc. The preceding information will provide you with survival knowledge and also give you the basis for your hunting strategy. Now you can analyze the map for features that might provide good hunting locations such as feeding areas, bedding sites, ridge trails, stream crossings or escape routes through funnel areas.

Always keep in mind that the compass needle can be deflected and give a false reading if you are near a metal object such as a firearm barrel, belt buckle or a vehicle. Be sure you hold your compass clear of such items while taking a reading.

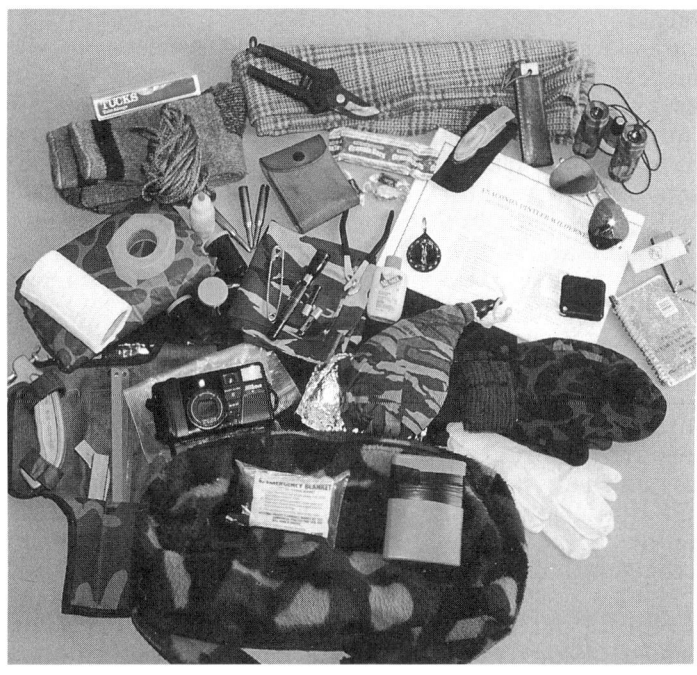

Some of these "day pack" items are carried in pockets.

Never leave camp without taking your day pack along, whether you are hunting, trailing game, scouting or just hiking. Experience will guide you as to the contents that you can comfortably carry. Your comfort relates to peace of mind enabling you to hunt far away areas combined with toting a lightweight pack. The contents will vary depending on the weather, the hunt conditions and the individual. For example, you will not need mosquito repellent in the winter or you would not carry spare ammunition while just hiking. Items that you might include in your day pack would be for survival, first aid, comfort or hunting.

For survival, you should always carry a spare knife, flashlight with extra batteries, spare compass, map, water, candy bars/food, rain gear, two types of fire starters, metal whistle, signal mirror, water purification tablets, roll of flagging, fishing line with hooks, signal flares, small nylon cord, space emergency blanket and several squares of tin foil. The fire starter can be waterproof matches in conjunction with a 35mm film canister filled with kerosene soaked sawdust or oiled steel wool. The backup can be a metal match or magnesium bar. The flagging can be used to mark your trail to assist you in survival navigation, trailing wounded game or to retrace your steps if you plan to return to retrieve game. The tin foil is a substitute for a cooking container.

For emergencies, a compact first aid kit needs to be carried in your pack or your jacket pocket.

For comfort, include a change of wool socks, a spare pair of wool hunting gloves, sunglasses, lip protection, insect repellent, some type of headache medicine and toilet paper.

Items that might be needed for hunting would be a collapsible saw with both bone and wood cutting blades, nylon ropes, binoculars, knife sharpener, spare ammunition, a small camera with built in flash and perhaps a small set of pulleys.

Finally, in the bottom of the pack, lay 1 or 2 large plastic bags which will have a multitude of uses from substitute rain gear to a liver bag. I always pack a bandanna and a wool scarf if I am not wearing them. The scarf can be used for an emergency wrap or an extra head warmer.

Be sure to practice with your equipment, especially the compass and fire starters, so that you are knowledgeable in their use and limitations. Some of this equipment can be carried in trouser or jacket pockets, on your belt or around your neck, while the remainder should always be in your knapsack or fanny pack.

If you do get lost, it is ineffective to fire three gun shots into the air, especially in a public hunting area. Unless this is done at night or in response to a search party signal, it will not attract rescue attention since it will simulate a hunting situation.

A whistle, using a series of three blasts, or an SOS signal is the best call for help. This would involve 3 quick blasts ("S"), 3 slow or long blasts ("O") and then 3 more quick ones ("S"). In lieu of a whistle, the sound of beating on a dead tree with a stick will carry a long way and the SOS signal repeated several times should be used.

The first thing to do when lost is to admit that you are lost and STOP. This is an acronym for *Sit, Think, Observe* and *Plan*. In other words, it is your mental survival kit. You must *Sit down* to stop yourself from continuing to walk. It also eases the panic and allows you to better *Think* over your situation. Try to recall any reference or datum from the origin of your hunt. Do you know if the access road is a N-S road or if it runs E-W? Are there any streams in the area that you can recall their flow direction or any points where they cross the road? Is there any geographic feature to help orient yourself? Did you notice the wind direction or your travel route when you left camp? If your decision is to spend the night in the woods, then you must turn your thoughts to comfort and survival. Your first priority is protection from the weather and a warm camp. A source of water is also an important factor since most people require 8 or more cups (2 quarts) of water daily. One serious indicator of dehydration is the color of urine, which will become progressively darker as a person becomes more dehydrated.

You will then need to *Observe* your surroundings and select the best site for a camp. Select an area where a campfire will keep you warm but will also be visible to a rescue party. Next, inventory all the items in your pockets and pack, plus check your ammunition supply.

Now you can *Plan* your survival. Depending on the circumstances, you can decide if you will need to wait in your emergency camp for rescue or if you can properly orient yourself to navigate out when daylight comes. If you have a proper map and compass, your physical condition is good and the weather allows it, you will likely be able to continue your route and hunt out as planned. Do this only if you are sure of your location. Under no circumstances, when lost, should you cross a road or continue to move. The rescue party will confine their search to within the road system where you were originally lost and would have no reason to search where you are not supposed to be. Also, they can not locate you if you continue to move and perhaps wander into an area that they have already thoroughly searched.

In the not too distant future, wilderness hunters might carry a Global Positioning System (GPS) and then they will never get lost. This system, designed for the military, and used by American troops in the Persian Gulf War, is a combination of

Wear hunter orange even while carrying deer out of the woods.

computer and satellite technology. A portable, hand-held unit, that cost about $3,000 four years ago when first marketed, is now available for less than $500. With three readings, you can establish exact latitude and longitude while a fourth reading will provide altitude. The more sophisticated units have built-in computer mapping capability with maps available for almost any place you want to hunt.

On the other hand, if one of your hunting companions is lost and you ask authorities for help, you will need to be able to describe certain information. You will need to know name, address, any medical problems, physical description of hunter, type of hunting equipment, outer clothing and footwear (especially boot tread pattern), location and time last seen plus destination of intended hunt.

Remember, survival is the responsibility of each hunter. Become familiar with the hunt area and when you leave your vehicle or start out from camp, take a compass bearing and be sure you have the proper equipment with you.

No amount of planning can ever replace dumb luck.

HUNTERS BEWARE!

When it comes to first aid in the field, a little knowledge can be a dangerous thing, but no knowledge at all is worse. This chapter will serve as an introduction to hunter's emergency first aid, hypothermia and lyme disease.

The first thing you should do when encountering a potential victim is to survey the scene to determine the cause of the accident and the extent of the injury. Then follow the first aid ABC's, which are:

AIRWAY—Be certain that the airway is open.

BREATHING—Check for chest movement and air escaping from mouth and nose.

CIRCULATION—Check for pulse, then control serious bleeding.

Without a constant supply of oxygen, the brain begins to die within 4-6 minutes. First, be sure to clear anything in victim's mouth and throat, using your fingers. With the victim on his back, tilt his head back with chin pointing up, jaw jutting out, and place your mouth tightly over victim's mouth, breathing air into him while pinching his nostrils shut. For an adult, breathe about 12 times per minute (once every 5 seconds) removing mouth each time to allow escape of air.

If victim is choking, and desires your assistance, perform the Heimlich Maneuver. Be aware that even if object is expelled, the irritated area may swell and shut off the air supply. In case you are hunting alone, and an object lodges in your throat, you can perform the Heimlich Maneuver on yourself using your fist, a stump, a railing, etc.

Just when you think it will never happen to you, it usually does, and this was the case during a wilderness drop hunt on the Alaskan Peninsula. Early in the hunt, while sharpening his knife with a hand held steel, my friend's knife skipped off the sharpener and sliced into his wrist causing heavy bleeding. We were able to stop the bleeding with direct pressure. Without removing the original cloth pad, several layers of blood soaked towels were required. It was my turn next, as I burned my hand and caught the wall of the cabin on fire with spilled fuel oil that I was using to help the rain soaked wood ignite. The closest liquid was a two day supply of soup which soon covered the wall, extinguishing the blaze. My burned hand healed quickly after immersion in cold water and a wrapping of clean cloth.

Knowledge to apply direct pressure to a wound, and, if possible, raising it above the victim's body, controls loss of blood. A tourniquet should be used only as a last resort to control life threatening bleeding, with the awareness that the victim will very likely lose the extremity.

For campfire burns, try to relieve the pain by keeping air away from the burn. For small burns, if skin is unbroken, and there are no blisters, immerse burned part in cold water or apply a cold pack. Bandage with layers of sterile gauze pad or clean cloth. If blisters occur, do not break them, but cover loosely with clean sterile cloth.

For broken bones, place the injured part in as natural a position as possible using a splint to prevent movement. The splint should extend well beyond the joint, above and below the fracture. If back or neck injury is suspected, do not move the patient unless absolutely necessary, and then only with full support of his entire body.

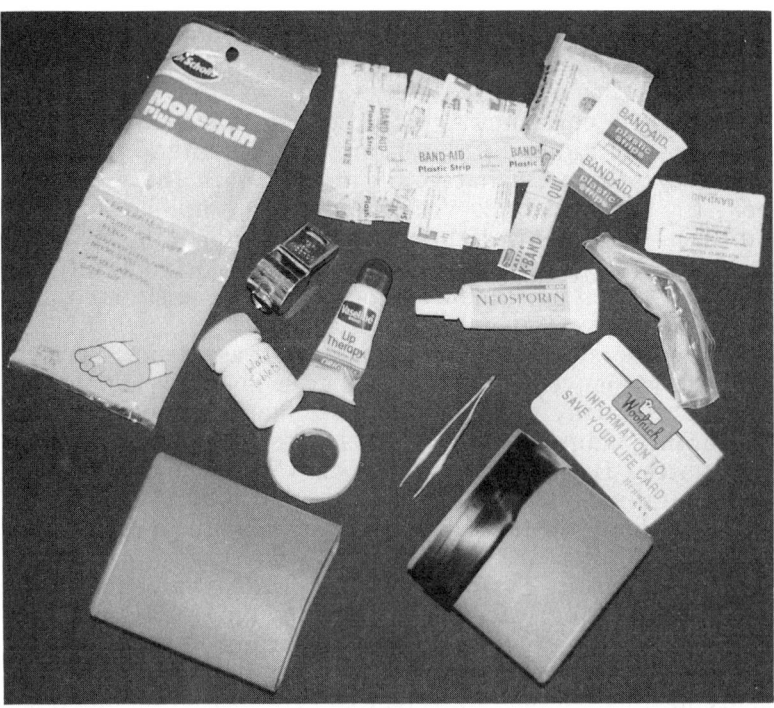

First aid kit including: moleskin, various bandaids and gauze, metal whistle, Neosporin, aspirin, water purification tablets, Vaseline, tweezers, adhesive tape, first aid booklet, and the plastic carrying case that is taped shut. Missing is personal emergency medicine.

A combination of conditions including accidents while hunting from a boat, wet clothing from moisture on bushes, excessive sweating, or hunting in the rain can lead to hypothermia. Hypothermia, which means lowered body temperature, is the silent killer. All hunters should be aware of hypothermia, plan for prevention, and be able to recognize its symptoms in other people. A person with hypothermia loses heat faster than his body can regenerate. It begins when you get wet and then become chilled and it can happen in temperatures of 40° to 60° Fahrenheit. The cold blood of your limbs circulates to your body core and brain, robbing your brain of oxygen and with it, your ability to comprehend your predicament. Initial symptoms would include shivering, and feelings of being cold. The victim should be removed from the cold conditions, dried, warmed and given warm liquids. In moderate cases, where slurred speech, stumbling, confusion and uncontrolled shivering occur, treat victim gently. Avoid exercise and warm victim while drying his clothes. When severe symptoms occur, professional care should be solicited. The victim will be unresponsive, with decreased pulse and respiration. Shivering may cease altogether and the person may totally collapse. Warmth should be provided to the body core areas of head, neck, armpit and groin with warmed blankets, warm water bottles or another warm body. A potentially fatal phenomenon called "after-drop" can occur if victim's limbs are warmed, forcing the cold blood back into the vitals, further lowering the core temperature.

To prevent hypothermia, stay dry, or if wet, get dry. Keep your body in good physical condition and pace yourself to avoid overexertion which can result in excessive sweating or fatigue.

It may not be easy for any of us who enjoy the out-of-doors to avoid contracting Lyme Disease. However, this disease can be treated in any of its three stages. Results show that earlier treatment will increase the chances of full recovery. Treatment consists of an antibiotic therapy with high enough levels to cleanse the bloodstream while reaching all of the affected body tissues.

The disease received its name when the bacteria was first recognized in the mid 1970's at Lyme, Connecticut. It is transmitted by the deer tick which is roughly half the size of the dog tick. The disease can be spread at almost any time during the two year life of the tick, but the greatest risk is during the warmer months of May through August.

A tick may take 6 to 12 hours to attach to its host. It will then feed for a period of 1 to 3 days or longer. Bacteria is passed to the host during the feeding period.

Lyme Disease usually involves three stages, but individual stages can overlap or be absent. In stage one, the victim may experience flu-like symptoms of headache, chills, fever, nausea and possibly aching joints. Accompanying these signs will normally be a telltale rash, originating at the source of the bite. About one third of the victims do not even exhibit this rash, which begins as a small red dot appearing on the skin within 3 to 30 days of the bite. The rash, often itchy or burning, can expand to an oval or irregular circle several inches across, as the bacteria spreads within the skin. Satellite red rashes on other areas of the skin may also appear. The center portion is usually a raised pale area resembling a bullseye, but it may also have the appearance of a blister. Further complicating the diagnosis, this rash often clears itself within an average of three weeks. This also gives the victim the false impression that he is cured.

During the second stage, which can occur weeks to months following exposure to the bacteria, complications to the heart and/or nervous system can occur. Painful joints, tendons or muscles may also be experienced.

One of the most commonly recognized final stages of Lyme Disease is arthritis. Untreated victims result in Lyme Arthritis in about half of the known cases. Large joints, rather than smaller ones, are primarily affected.

The two best methods of prevention for hunters are a repellent and an examination of the body after a hunt. Odor free repellents containing Diethyltoluamide (DEET) are available. Some labels warn that this chemical should be applied to pants, socks and boots only, and contact with the skin should be avoided. Following a hunt, check your clothes and then thoroughly bathe while checking your body carefully for ticks, especially in hairy areas. In this way you can locate them and they can be removed before they embed. To remove an attached tick, grasp it with tweezers, as close to the skin as possible, and using a firm, constant effort, gently pull it straight out. Cleanse the bite area and your hands with soap and water and then apply an antiseptic to the bite. If a portion of the tick's head remains embedded, or if suspicion of lyme disease is present, save the tick body and consult a physician.

Blood tests, which will reveal your body's natural antibodies, are available to detect the presence of the lyme bacteria. At the time of this writing, a vaccine for domestic animals and humans has been developed and is being tested. Undoubtedly, several years of testing will be required before it will be available to the public.

For further information and a free brochure on Lyme Disease, you can contact the National Arthritis Foundation, P.O. Box 19000, Atlanta, Ga. 30326, or your local arthritis chapter.

"Clothes make the man. Naked people have little or no influence in society."
Mark Twain

CLOTHES FOR THE HUNTER

Select clothing for safety, comfort, quiet moving and concealment. Think safety first, especially during the firearm season.

For greatest safety you should always wear orange up high providing you with your best visibility. This is especially true when you are moving. While on stand, I often change my hunter orange hat to camouflage whenever regulations allow it. This minimizes the movement of my hunter orange clothing since my head will be moving more than any other part. Of course my hunter orange vest, meeting the regulations, will be kept on at all times. Do not be lulled into a sentimental error by using the hunter orange vest that you bought ten years ago. The color fades and gets stained over the years and the garment may not even look orange anymore. It may even appear brown at a distance and could be mistaken for a deer in the brush. Never wear white clothes for hunting unless it is a camo snow outfit when there is total snow cover. Solid hunter orange is more visible than the camo orange and consequently it is the only allowable outer wear in many states where a hunter orange regulation exists. Be certain that whatever hunter orange you wear, it is clearly visible from any direction.

The trick to being warm and comfortable is to keep dry by wicking the moisture away from your skin. Wool, polypropylene and silk undergarments provide this wicking effect and they all dry fairly quickly when removed. When temperatures or exertion will vary greatly during a day, layering provides the flexibility to add or remove clothing as required so that you do not perspire as you retain body heat. The most important item for cold weather hunting goes on first. It is the undergarment. While it is difficult to keep pace with technology, I can assure you that after you spend the extra money for the double or triple layered underwear with wool, polypropylene or some other synthetic, you will never regret your investment. Ask for a set for Christmas.

When hunting, allow time to walk slowly into your stand and set up with minimum exertion. Stop often if it is a long uphill walk. If necessary, remove hat, scarf, gloves and jacket to keep from perspiring. Open your shirt and leave it untucked for ventilation.

On one early season bow hunt, my only stand approach was through several fields of weeds and soybeans that were waist high and heavy with dew. I hate to be on stand with wet clothing if I can help it, so in an attempt to keep dry, I slipped a waterproof plastic rain suit over my hunting pants. As it turned out the pants were extremely noisy and I had to remove the rain gear to complete my silent approach to the stand, choosing wet over noise.

If you analyze your body like a radiator and adequately insulate your arms and legs, you can more effectively keep your hands and feet warm. Body heat will reach these extremities if it is not allowed to escape enroute. This analogy works, but you also have to have the proper protection for your hands and feet.

A change of wool socks or spare hunting gloves can be a welcome relief when your original set gets wet or even moist making the resulting dampness cold and uncomfortable. It always seems that if I can just keep my feet warm, my whole body stays warm.

One winter for stand hunting, I tried electric socks. Since they used "C" cell batteries, I bought a flashlight that also used two "C" cells. When I got to the stand, using my flashlight, I switched the batteries into my socks. My heels got warm but my toes froze.

A few years ago, I tried my first pair of polypropylene socks and now wear them under my wool socks on the coldest days. This synthetic fabric does an excellent job of wicking the moisture away from us sweaty footed hunters.

Boot selection depends almost entirely on the type of hunting that you will be doing that day. Be certain that your boots have adequate support or they can cause you to tire more quickly. For cold weather stands, it is hard to beat felt pac boots with their rubber soles and leather uppers. Use the thicker 3/8" felt liners and be sure to take a spare pair to camp for daily rotation allowing one pair to dry thoroughly. This dual supply also holds true for the felt pads used in leather boots. Gore-Tex/thinsulate liners are also available, and provide a lightweight waterproof insulation system. For standers, 800 grams of thinsulate is great, but for a walking hunter 400 to 200 grams is better. Leather boots with the Gore-Tex waterproof lining or the addition of thinsulate to the Gore-Tex membrane provide a waterproof or an insulated waterproof boot. These lightweight models, with an adequate cleat for traction, are deservedly very popular, especially for stillhunting. New leather boots may squeak, but well oiled boots are the quietest footwear. Oil base waterproofing will only work on oil tanned boots, while dry tanned boots must be treated only with silicone. Soft soles are necessary for proper stalking, so the hunter can feel sticks or loose stones before breaking or dislodging them.

Bowhunters, concerned with depositing their scent, prefer rubber soles or complete rubber boots, insulated or not, that do not allow human odors to pass through to the trail.

When trying on boots, think winter, and wear two pairs of socks so that you select a pair large enough for cold weather hunting without being too tight on your toes. Your best fit will be tight at the ankle for support, snug at the heel and loose enough at the toes for good blood circulation.

My main winter hunting problem is keeping my hands warm, especially during the late bow season. I solved this by making myself a wooly bully. This item consists of unshorn sheepskin with 3" long hairs, sewn into a pouch and inserted into another pouch made from fleece camo material that I suspend on my belt. Now, while hunting, I have to take my hand, with release, out of the pouch occasionally to let it cool.

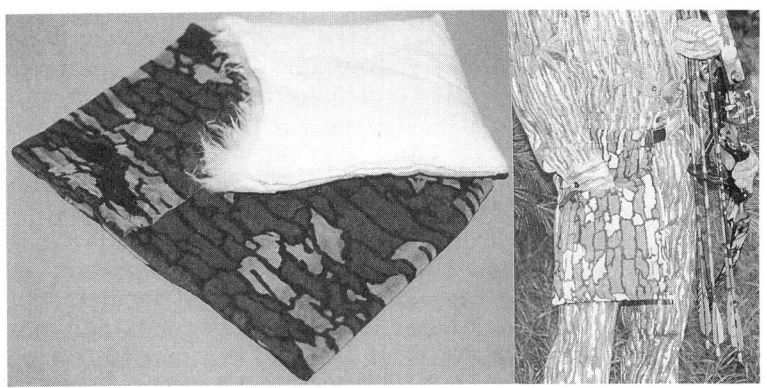

The wooly bully sheepskin pouch.

When on stand in cold weather, I often use mittens. They are much warmer than gloves and I have never missed an opportunity for a shot in the time it takes to remove the mitten from my shooting hand. If you are moving, or in a hunting situation where you might jump a deer, a glove that permits a quick shot would be a better choice.

With the invention of Gore-Tex, many hunters have changed their hunting tactics. Now we can hunt in the rain all day and stay dry and comfortable using Gore-Tex rain gear. Although this new rain gear does breathe, it will not provide sufficient ventilation quickly enough during strenuous hunting activity. The woodland camo Gore-Tex rain gear I purchased has short wool fibers for the outer layer so it is also quiet. The Gore-Tex membrane is waterproof and a good wind break. For cold weather hunting, an added thinsulate material with a thickness of 200 grams also gives you insulation under the waterproof layer while maintaining a lightweight product. A goose down or some other insulated vest will maintain body heat while allowing good ventilation. On a hunt where you will have some exertion, such as in mountainous terrain, a vest is popular and can be worn over a wool shirt or under the Gore-Tex rain gear. If you purchase one, select the vest that provides the longest back to eliminate lower back drafts.

Overall, wool outer clothes provide the quietest, most versatile hunting garments, since wool continues to insulate even when wet. Some of the new materials, such as cotton chamois or the cotton/polyester brushed twill can be as quiet as wool but few can match its wear strength. A brushed cotton fabric makes a good warm weather hunting outfit.

Your hunting hat is an extremely important clothing item. Most hunters will use several types during the season, depending on the weather. An orange hat may be the safest, but keep in mind, it is the first part of you over the ridge, and could alert game prematurely. In early bowhunting season, a well ventilated hat, with a brim, is the best combination. The brim shades the sun, shadows the hunter's face and helps protect it from wind and rain. If you are hunting and it begins to rain, use a plastic bag the size of a bread sack, under your hat extending over your jacket collar to keep your head dry. As the weather gets cooler and body heat needs to be retained, a Gore-Tex/thinsulate or insulated hat should be worn. In cold weather, I like a Gore-Tex/thinsulate camouflage hunting hat. This hat is warm and waterproof but also breathes, so my head is well insulated but dry. In extremely cold weather, the combination hat/face mask or balaclava will keep you warm on stand. This item is designed with a polypropylene lining under a camo wool exterior.

The one most ignored cold weather piece of clothing is the scarf. A simple piece of plaid, tight knit wool about a foot wide and six feet long works great. It can be used effectively to hold body heat in around your neck while tucked into your jacket. I use it in lieu of a turtleneck, since I can unwrap or remove it quickly when I want to cool down. If nobody is watching and your face is cold, do what the local "bag lady" does and scarf up, by wrapping it around your chin and head.

When it comes to hot seats, I have tried every type from a homemade square of rubber backed carpet tied onto my belt to the jumbo manufactured plastic ones. It is nice to be able to sit comfortably with a dry seat and I appreciate this addition to hunting gear while on a ground stand. I prefer the nylon hot seats since they can be repacked with styrofoam to bulk them back to their original shape. Also, I have had the plastic ones produce an ominous squeak as I pivoted on my seat for a shot, only to have the quarry spook and run.

Now that we are safe, dry and comfortable, let us try to hide. The single most important aspect of concealment is to remain motionless. Since that is almost impossible, your next best line of defense is to conceal the parts of your body that might move, and finally, try to hide your overall silhouette since any movement will attract the games' attention.

The modern hunter has the opportunity to select a camouflage outfit that will blend with almost any surrounding. Camo patterns range from a leafy material to a tree bark like material all the way up to limbs silhouetted in the sky, and many combinations of these. It is not important to match your camo outfit. In fact, if hunting from a tree stand, the use of a pattern that looks like the bark of a tree on your pants, topped by a leafy or brushy type jacket and hat, will help to break up the human shape. While turkey hunting, I often reverse this by using leafy pants or coveralls covered by a jacket and hat with a tree bark material while sitting on the ground with my back to a tree. This outfit would also be effective while deer hunting from a ground blind.

Covering your head and neck for concealment with a loose fitting face mask can help keep mosquitoes and other insects from bothering you. Using a face net also works fine for short periods and a mask with eye holes permits the hunter to adequately see his sights. Since a mask holds some heat in, face paint would be cooler. If you plan to hunt all day or desire to be more thoroughly camouflaged, paint your head and hands. When I say head, be sure to include your neck, ears and even your eyelids. Also, the backs of your hands should get plenty of attention. Remember, the most important parts to hide are the ones in motion. If you prefer gloves, make certain that they cover your wrist, especially if you are wearing a wrist watch.

On the ground, insert a sprig into your quiver to hide the bow and break up the silhouette of the hunter.

Most manufactures of camouflage clothing have designed

their clothing to be worn in a shadow, so, try to avoid direct sunlight in your set up and use the natural shadows to their best advantage. Never forget that your shadow is not camo, and be especially careful when the sun is near the horizon and you are projecting a long shadow. In selecting your clothing, stick to name brands that you have some knowledge about or experience with. Check with friends who have worn their camo outfits for several years. Beware of a bargain that fades after several washes and a little exposure. Recently, hunters have discovered that ultraviolet (UV) brighteners exist in some fabrics and these garments will spook deer even when the hunter is not moving. A good camo pattern must have contrast and bold colors or they will become solid shapes, silhouetting the hunter, when viewed at distances of 40 yards or more. When selecting your hunting pants, consider the carrying capacity of the pockets. Be certain that they are large, deep and can keep the contents secure. Archers should beware when purchasing a jacket or shirt that the pocket flaps or snaps do not interfere with their bow string upon release. For foul weather or stand hunting, coveralls or bib overalls are desirable. My wife has added 18" leg zippers to several pairs of bibs so that they are more convenient to remove over hunting boots.

A good hunting technique, if you have access to the proper water, is stream stillhunting. Over your waterproof waders or hip boots, wear your camo hunting clothes. This allows quiet stream walking while staying dry. It is especially effective during bow season for close encounters.

Be selective when making your clothing purchases. It can be as critical as your bow or firearm for a successful hunting season.

"Happiness is . . . wanting what you get."
Anonymous

FINDING A NEEDLE IN A HAYSTACK

Finding a whitetail shed, or cast, antler in the woods can be as difficult as finding a needle in a haystack, but it can also be exciting. It is especially rewarding if you are scouting and shed hunting.

Generally, the best time to shed hunt is after Valentines Day, however, as early as January a buck can drop his antlers. Most of the sheds that I have found have been in March or April. Some of the bucks that I have bumped while scouting in mid-March have still been wearing their adornments. In *The Deer of North America*, Leonard Lee Rue III notes that the use of testosterone and the diminished activity of the pituitary gland due to decreased number of daylight hours causes the antlers to drop off. When the testosterone level drops, a layer of cells at the base of the antler granulates and the antler drops away at the pedicel. The largest strongest bucks do most of the breeding, and therefore drop their antlers earliest.

Unclaimed trophy found in the spring while shed hunting.

During March, in my area, the freshly shed antlers still have dark stains and are difficult to spot on the ground. Later, during April, before the undergrowth conceals them, they bleach white and are more easily located. Unfortunately, squirrels and other animals also see them easier and the late sheds that you find are often chewed on. Since rodents and other animals gnaw antlers, they normally remain intact for only a few weeks. Deer also have been known to chew on the antlers cast by themselves or others to obtain minerals which their body needs. Sheds in open areas and fields seem to remain the longest.

To properly hunt sheds you must change your hunting tactics. Instead of a glance down at the trail in front of you along with a study of the terrain ahead, you must glance ahead and then study the ground all around you. Hunting habits are hard to break and invariably you will cover some ground with barely a downward glance.

5-point shed found in grass along trail through pines. Shed 4-point found in bedding area.

Due to the shape of an antler, it will usually lay with its tines up, making it hard to identify in grassy areas. Since it has an irregular shape, you cannot look for just the tines but must search for the entire antler.

With this much attention to details on the ground, it will surprise you what other treasures you could find. While shed hunting, I have found knives, grunt calls, arrows, a trail timer, scent dispensers and a metal knife sharpener. Also, each spring I find several unclaimed dead deer, including some bucks with their antlers still intact. For this reason, I carry a small collapsible bone saw to salvage the antlers.

Bucks will kick off the annoying loose antlers with their hind foot. They usually remove their antlers in an area where they are relaxed. That is why most sheds are found in or near a bedding area or in wide spaces along trails. Grassy lanes through which trails pass are my favorite spots to search.

While I always hope to find both sheds together, this usually does not occur. They can easily be shed a long distance apart since they are often dropped on different days.

Sheds provide a good indicator of the bucks that have survived both hunting season and the worst of the winter. They are often found in areas where the buck frequents. This may well be his "home" or core area where he will spend most of his time.

Orientals grind antlers into a powder that is used to make an aphrodisiac (sex stimulant). Since I do not have that formula, mine are used for decorations, knife handles, buttons or occasionally to repair a broken tine on a set of antlers that are not to be measured for the record book.

Matching 8-points found in March. One was still in thornapple tree!

Even if your travels do not produce sheds, it is still a good spring leg exercise and an excellent time to scout winter deer trails.

> *"A lazy man won't even dress the game he gets while hunting, but the diligent man makes good use of everything he finds."*
> Proverbs 12:27

CARING FOR YOUR DEER

From the woods to the palate, every step affects the taste, tenderness and desirability of venison. It is not the clean outdoor lifestyle, nor the animals diet that gives deer a "gamey" flavor, but the improper handling prior to meeting the cook. Through my own experiences plus knowledge gained from association with other hunters I have learned a great deal about the care of deer. Let's take the procedures in order and perhaps you will find some new ideas that will allow you to enjoy your deer even more.

As little time as possible should elapse between your well placed shot and recovery of your deer. Immediately start field dressing to cool the meat. This should include removing paunch, reproductive organs, intestines, diaphragm, liver, heart and lungs, plus accumulated blood. The only remaining parts inside will be the tenderloins. Be careful not to spill the always full bladder while removing it. Stop your belly cut at the rib cage for now. After tagging, move the deer to camp or wherever it will hang. If transporting in a vehicle, protect it from heat and dirt and for everyone's sake it is also best to keep it out of sight so we do not offend non-hunters. After the deer is hung, continue cleaning and cooling. This will include cutting through the rib cage and splitting the neck skin to the head while removing the wind pipe. If you intend to have a head mount, cape the animal prior to the last step. Simply stated: if it is hot weather, remove the skin, if it isn't, leave it on until you are ready to butcher. Next, remove interior fat and trim any damaged portions that are bruised or bloody. Both fat and blood will spoil meat and are undesirable. Caution: if tagging, dragging and hanging will take more than a couple of hours, this cleaning procedure will not wait, especially in hot weather. While deer still has body heat, it is a good time to wash off blood and any intestinal material that has leaked from shot or field dressing. Add four tablespoons of white vinegar to a 2 liter plastic bottle and fill with water. This is handy to carry in your vehicle and will help dissolve blood, making cleaning easier. After the deer has cooled, keep all moisture off the carcass since it will accelerate meat spoilage. Be careful to keep dirt and particularly hair out of cavity and off the meat during processing. Always split skin from the inside (blade pointed out) using a very sharp knife to minimize cutting deer hair.

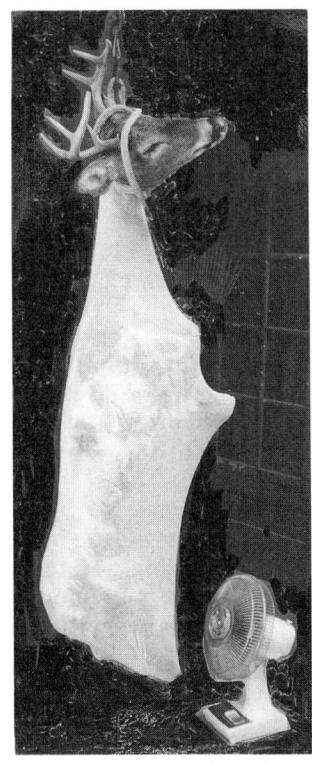

Game bag and fan.

In camp, skinning may not be practical since the hide will protect the meat from dehydration, dirt, insects and weather, shedding rain if deer is hung by head. After splitting rib cage and neck, prop the body cavity open to allow air to circulate. In warm weather your deer will attract insects, but an application of black pepper will discourage egg laying flies. When possible, I use a fan blowing on skinned deer to keep flies from landing. If it is a hot day, the addition of a gallon jug of frozen water suspended in the body cavity will help the meat cool. A cheesecloth game bag, tightly tied, with ice jug in cavity, and fan blowing, may be required, and this simple arrangement works very well. Limit this procedure to a day or two to prohibit air drying of meat. If you have a walk-in cooler or perfect 40° weather, it will not hurt to hang your deer for a week or more. This will allow a biological decomposition from the inside, tenderizing the meat. Many hunters do not feel that this aging process is necessary for fine flavored tender venison. Others package their meat and then leave it in the refrigerator for a couple of days, prior to freezing.

If you decide to save the hide, remove all fat and meat (fleshing) and sprinkle with 1-2 pounds of salt to draw out moisture. Tanned and dyed buckskin can be used to make personal gifts for friends and family.

Author fleshes deer hide with help from "Midnight" and "Tawny."

Most of us who butcher our own deer, completely bone out the meat, trimming all fat, sinew (tendons), veins and tissue. I seldom cut steaks while butchering, but instead, separate the ribeye (back strap) from one side of the backbone and divide it into thirds.

When packaged, it is labeled ribeye—back, middle or front, with the back being the prime cut. When thawed, it can be cut into the number of steaks desired. The round gets similar packaging but usually ends up as a roast. Carefully label packages since various cuts of steaks and roasts cook differently.

For burgers, store the trimmed, cut up pieces of venison in refrigerator overnight. Prior to grinding, drain off any blood that has seeped out. This will help the flavor of your burger tremendously. Buy some beef fat (suet) and after trimming, grind about 1 pound of suet with 6-10 pounds of lean venison as desired. I have tried using deer fat with mixed results and no longer take the risk. The flavor of deer fat somehow depends on the age, sex and diet of the deer.

Products from processed deer skin.

After wrapping, dating and labeling the meat, place in freezer. In the past, I always double wrapped with freezer paper to protect from freezer burn, but recently, especially with burger, I have switched to quart plastic freezer bags. In freezer, do not stack fresh meat, but separate on shelves, allowing uniform freezing of each package. Deep stacking could insulate center packages which would begin decomposing prior to freezing. Oh yes! If you are permitted to butcher in the kitchen please clean up your mess thoroughly.

To thaw, remove burger one day ahead and a roast or steak two days ahead of cooking and place in refrigerator. Slower thawing maintains higher moisture in meat and keeps it from getting tough. Soak whole meat in water in the refrigerator the second day. This will remove blood carrying enzymes and enhance the flavor. This soaking process is especially important if animal was stressed by shot or other circumstances while still alive.

Whether you are cooking venison burger, roast, steak or crock pot meat for your dinner, you have a treat in store. The hunter and the cook, if other than the hunter, work in conjunction for this effort. Proper care in the field will result in the tastiest venison throughout the year.

Tools required

BUTCHERING YOUR DEER

The following photographs demonstrate a step by step procedure for home butchering. All you need is a bone saw, cutting board and a very sharp butcher knife. My butchering philosophy, simply stated, is, "If it is white, get it out." In other words, remove all fat, bones, tendons, membranes and sinew from the meat.

This gourmet meat falls below the American Heart Association's guidelines for calories, fat and cholesterol, while containing no hormones.

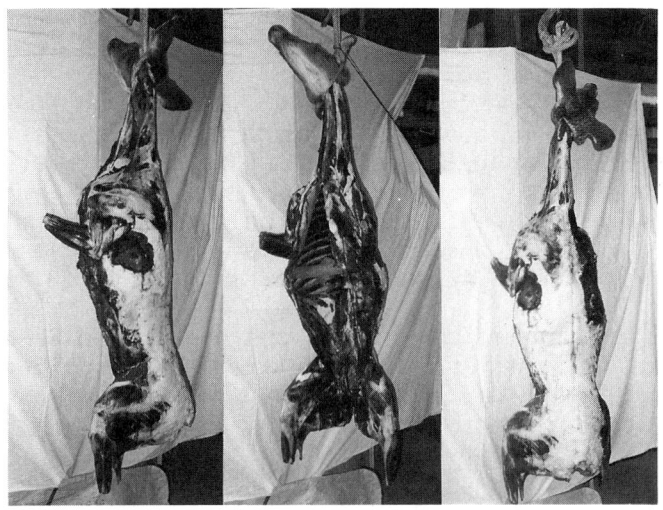

Side, Front, and Back view of skinned deer

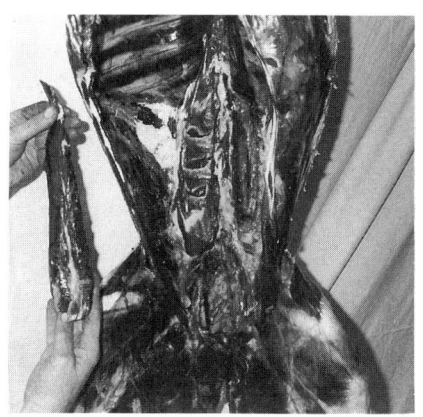

One tenderloin removed, one remaining inside body cavity.

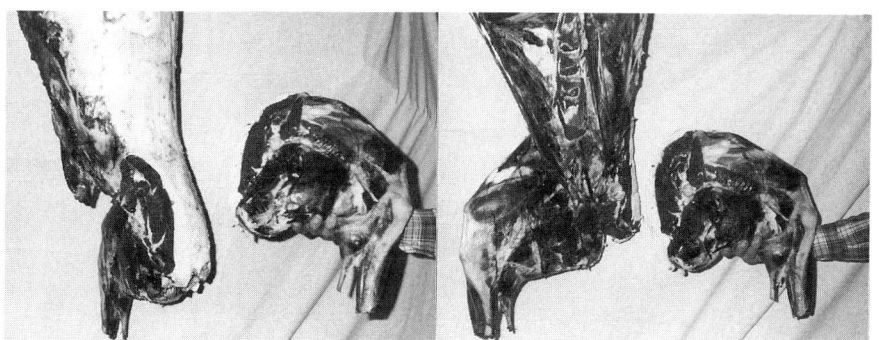

One back leg removed at socket joint.

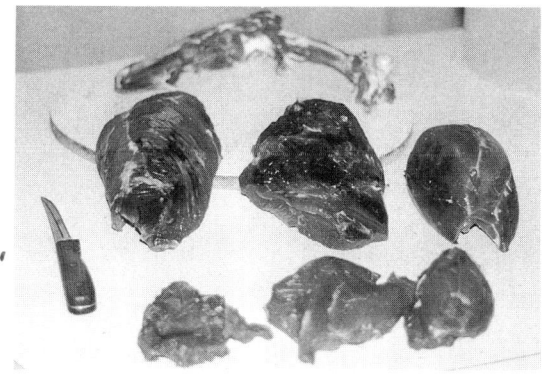

Two round roasts (top left), heel of round (top right), and trimmings from one back leg. Separate the major muscles by using the membrane between them after cutting meat free from the bone.

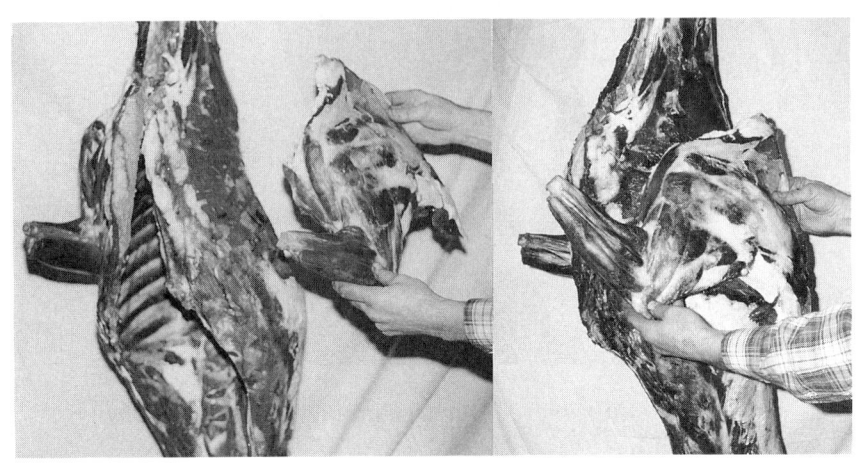

Cut through muscles to free one front leg from carcass

After cutting meat free from the bone, trim for stew or burger

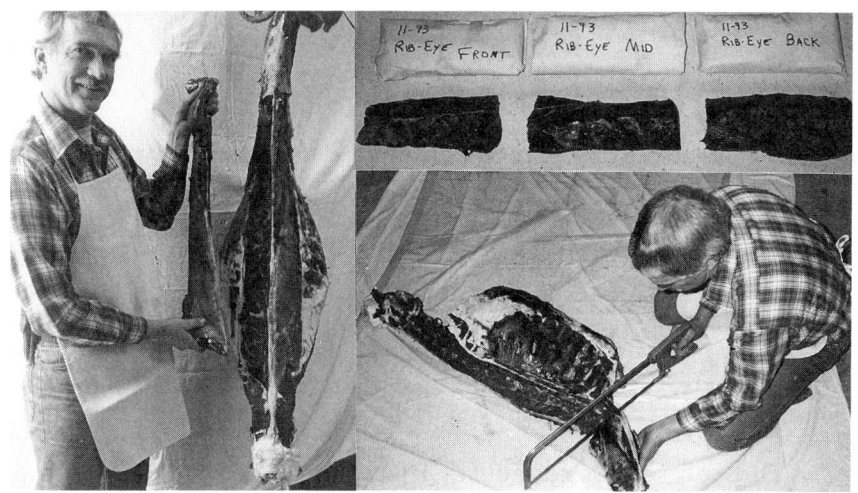

With all legs removed, cut off one full backstrap (ribeye) from base of neck roast to lower back, by sliding knife blade along spine and top of ribs. Separate backstrap into three segments, wrap and label. Remove neck roast after trimming all salvagable meat from carcass.

Grind burger with a 1 to 8 mixture of trimmed beef fat (suet) (1# suet to 8# meat). Coarse grind both, mix, and then fine grind together for best results. Burger is bagged in one pound packages.

*If guns cause crime, then
flies cause garbage.*

VENISON HOME CANNING

Over the years, I have searched for better ways to share venison with friends. The one meat that I consider superior to any other meat requires experience to prepare. Normally the small amount that you give to friends does not receive the proper cooking care. For example: a roast is too dry, a steak too tough, or the venisonburger has a cooking aroma that beef eaters are not accustomed to. Although you try to emphasize that a steak must be cooked very hot and served pink, newcomers to wild game feel protective by overcooking and therein lies the problem. You should probably tell them that it is only necessary to kill a deer once.

Through several references I have turned back the clock and learned to can venison. Besides reducing the load on the freezer, this provides an excellent precooked gift. It also produces meat to take to hunting camp without the need of a cooler. A local retired butcher has been an influence but the best written reference came from *The Readers Digest* publication "Back to Basics."

I prefer the raw "Cold Pack" method using sterilized wide mouth pint jars as the container since the meat is easier to pack and remove. To sterilize jars, boil for 10 minutes while completely filled and covered with water. You can pack a little more than one pound of meat per pint. Normally I use the venison round, cut into 1/2" to 3/4" strips about 2" long, with all fat and sinew removed. Meat is loosely packed into the sterilized jars to 1/2" from the top. To pint jars add 1/2 teaspoon of salt. Even though I wash the venison prior to canning, I add one tablespoon of water. Extra liquid does not hurt since later it will make great gravy. Place the uncovered jars in an open container with a couple inches of water and heat for an hour or so until the temperature in the middle of the meat reaches 170° F. This process, called exhausting, will drive out the air (watch the water level carefully). Prior to capping, tap jars to remove air and wipe top of glass to remove any particles. Firmly tighten sterilized lids and place jars into pressure cooker for canning. Leave a space between jars, make sure you have about 2" of water in canner and follow pressure cooker instructions carefully, especially the 10 minute exhausting period at the beginning. To kill bacteria in pint jars that could cause botulism, the meat must be treated for one hour and fifty minutes (110 minutes) at 240° F which equates to 10 pounds pressure in cooker. Old timers would simply place a 10 pound rock on canner lid to accomplish this pressure. After cooking the required time, remove jars and re-tighten lids as required.

Caution; if lid fails to seal, either discard contents or reprocess immediately. During storage, if lid bulges or leaks, discard where contents will not be eaten by an animal or another person.

Date and label jar after cooling. A simple ribbon around the lid makes a perfect gift. It takes a little extra time to can but no further cooking is required and the unique flavor justifies the effort. A favorite dish is Stroganoff but the canned venison is equally tasty with vegetables.

Mary Jane processing venison.

Venison Stroganoff

1 Large onion, chopped
2 Tbsp Butter
1 Cube chicken or beef bouillon, diluted to make one cup
¼ tsp Salt
¼ tsp Pepper
1 Pint canned Venison
1 Can Cream of Mushroom Soup
½ Cup sour cream

Saute onion in butter, add remaining ingredients and heat. If desired, thicken with flour. Serve over noodles (or rice). Serves 4.

*It is fortunate to have federal
lands where a hunter can roam
all day without trespassing.*

EXTENDING THE VENISON SEASON

After the hunt is over and you have told everybody who will listen, about your successful hunt, you may want to reread this chapter. Over the years many efforts have been made to produce the best jerky, summer sausage and stuffed sausage, so the venison can be shared, the audiences recaptured and the hunting stories retold. New recipes for venison are always welcomed by our family. Try some of the following ideas, modified, if necessary, to suit your taste and extend your venison season too.

Venison Jerky

1-2 # venison steak
¼ tsp salt
¼ tsp garlic powder
¼ tsp freshly ground black pepper

Trim all fat, cut meat lengthwise (with grain) into 1/8" thick strips. To cut this thin, partially frozen meat works best. Combine spices and sprinkle over meat. Go easy with your spices since it is common to over apply. Place strips on wax covered paper plates and cover with wax paper. Microwave at medium low heat (20-30% power) for 20 minutes. Remove, invert strips, change paper and plates as required, resalt, and cook at medium low heat another 20 minutes or until dry but slightly pliable. Meat takes a dark color with whiteness from salt. Often a thicker slice will take additional cooking. You can cook at higher power for proportionally shorter periods but the slower cooking allows more even cooking of uneven strips. If necessary, mix additional spices. To store, place in airtight container or store in the refrigerator.

Venison jerky in microwave.

Venison Summer Sausage

2½ # lean ground venison
1 tsp mustard seed
1 tsp black pepper
¼ tsp garlic powder
1½ Tbsp curing salt
1½ tsp liquid smoke
½ tsp onion salt
1 cup water

If a small amount of fat is mixed into your venison burger, it is ok. Mix all ingredients well, cover, and refrigerate. Mix several times a day for three days. Shape into five rolls with 2" diameter, about 5" long and place on broiling pan to catch drippings. Bake at 300° for 2-2 1/2 hours. Turn each hour. Cool, wrap in plastic and refrigerate. Wrap in freezer paper to freeze. Cut thin and serve with Ritz crackers.

Friends enjoying venison sausage at camp. Gary Melton, Tim McCurdy, Don Moore and Ben Parker.

Stuffed Venison Sausage

8# lean ground venison
2# bacon ends (fatty bacon)
2 cups water
½ cup salt
3 Tbsp black pepper

1 Tbsp mustard seed
2 Tbsp garlic powder
3 tsp sage
1 tsp onion powder
hog or collagen casings

Grind meats together, combine all ingredients and mix thoroughly. Grind through fine (1/8") plate and stuff casings. Twist or tie into 4"-5" links. Cook in 170° water until internal temperature reaches 152°. Immediately immerse in ice cold water, blot dry and refrigerate. Use plastic bags to freeze in packages of 6 to 8 links. This is great around the campfire at next year's hunting camp.

Hopefully, you have all the burger recipes that you need for meatloaf, lasagna, chili, spaghetti and tacos, so only two burger specialties will be listed. A roast is my favorite way to serve venison to company and this infallible recipe will make them think you are a gourmet cook. The Swiss steak dinner is a good method of cooking tougher cuts of deer but it is also fantastic with your best ribeye. Finally, I wanted to share variable uses of crock pot meat.

Venison Meat Balls
(Hors d'oeuvre)

1# venison burger
¼ cup whole milk
1 med. onion minced
½ tsp salt
¼ cup bread crumbs

1 cup flour
3 Tbsp butter
½ tsp thyme
3 Tbsp maple syrup
3 Tbsp vinegar
3 Tbsp prepared mustard
1/3 cup ketchup

Mix the first five ingredients and roll into 50 small meat balls (count them!). Dust with flour. Melt butter in iron skillet and brown meatballs. Remove meatballs and stir in remaining ingredients. Bring sauce to a boil, add meatballs and simmer for 12 minutes, stirring occasionally. Can be kept warm in oven until ready to serve. Bring toothpicks. (From a recipe by John Weiss)

Old Fashioned Meat Pie

1# venison burger
4 med. carrots—cut into ¼" slices
3 med. potatoes cubed
1 med. onion chopped
¼ cup flour
¼ cup water
1 tsp thyme
½ tsp garlic powder
2 tsp Worcestershire sauce
½ tsp salt
¼ tsp pepper

Brown meat. Place vegetables in pressure cooker, add 2" of water and cook for 10 minutes. Add meat. Make thickening with remaining ingredients. Shake until smooth and add to meat mixture. Cook until thickened and pour into 10" deep dish pie plate. Cover with biscuit mix while still hot and bake in hot oven at 400°-450° for 12-15 minutes. Serve promptly. Serves 4-6.

Biscuits

2 cups sifted—all purpose flour
2½ tsp baking powder
½ tsp salt
¼ cup shortening
2/3 cup milk (as needed)

Sift dry ingredients into mixing bowl. Cut in shortening until mixture texture resembles corn meal. Make a well in the center, add milk, stir quickly to blend. Add more milk if mixture seems dry. Mixture should leave sides of bowl, soft but not sticky. Turn onto lightly floured board. Knead about 10 strokes. Roll or pat into desired thickness—1/2" to 3/4". Cut with floured cutter and place on top of hot meat pie. Place leftovers on cookie sheet to cook separately.

Venison Roast

2-3# venison roast
1 can mushroom soup (substitute beefy-mushroom)
1 can French onion soup (substitute 1 cup red cooking wine)
1 pint tomato juice
½ stick margarine (1/8#)
¼ tsp garlic powder
¼ tsp black pepper
1 tsp salt

½ tsp sweet basil
4 large onions
4 large potatoes
8 large carrots

Brown venison using shortening, pour off any unwanted fat. Add soups, wine, juice and margarine. Cook covered for an hour at low heat (200°-225°). Add cut up potatoes, onions and carrots. Sprinkle on spices. Cook covered for 3 hours or until tender (200°-225°). Serves 4-6.

Venison roast with accompanying vegetables.

Venison Swiss Steak Dinner

1½-2# venison steak (round or ribeye)
1 med. onion—sliced
1 can French onion soup

Cut meat into 1" thick slices. Pound lightly with meat mallet, and coat with a mixture of:
1 cup flour
½ tsp garlic powder
½ tsp salt
½ tsp black pepper

Brown in hot oil in iron kettle. Add onion slices, pour in soup and add 1/2 can of water. Cover and cook in a slow oven at 300°

for 3-4 hours. Serve with mashed potatoes, using meat sauce for gravy. Include either green beans or corn as a side. Yum-yum!

Crock Pot Venison

To prepare venison for the crock pot, begin by trimming off all fat and sinew. Next, cut meat into small chunks and soak in water in the refrigerator overnight. Drain water and place meat into crock pot with a couple of tablespoons of water per pound of meat. Slow cook covered 4-5 hours until meat falls apart, stirring occasionally. Add one can of French onion soup for every 1 to 1 1/2 pounds of venison, replace cover and slow cook for another hour. I normally crock pot about three pounds of venison at a time with two cans of soup, and this provides the basis for several meals as follows:

First meal	—Plain meat on a bun,
Second meal	—Add barbecue sauce to enough meat for several sandwiches.
Third meal	—Cook noodles for a venison/noodle dinner.
Left overs	—Use any remaining meat to make venison stew or vegetable soup.

With the meat precooked, all of these simple recipes are great to take to camp so more time can be spent hunting.

Steak Salad

For the diet conscious hunter, a steak salad may be just the answer. Surprisingly, it is a very satisfying meal. Tender strips of venison steak 1/2" wide and 3" long are cooked and simply placed on top of a large tossed salad. The salad is prepared to include your favorite vegetables mixed with an abundance of cut up lettuce and spinach leaves. A small amount of dressing and a couple of hard rolls complete the main course. Initially, I was skeptical of this meal as a complete dinner, but now I am a convert and list this salad as one of my favorite summertime menus.

APPENDIX

Article reprinted from the
April 1986 issue of
"Outdoor Indiana" magazine,
Indiana Department of
Natural Resources.

HOW TO AGE INDIANA DEER

DNR biologist explains how to determine a whitetail's age

By Ed Guljas

One of the greatest challenges encountered by the deer hunter, after he bags a deer and figures out how to get it back to his vehicle, is determining the age of the deer. Some say they can tell the age of a whitetail by how much the deer weighs. Others say the best way to tell a buck's age is by the number of points on the antlers. Don't believe it. These characteristics vary from year to year and from deer to deer. There is one sure-fire way of telling a deer's age and it has to do with the teeth. The old adage about not looking a gift horse in the mouth certainly does not apply to deer.

Those who do not pursue deer may wonder why anyone would want to know how old a deer is. Hunters know the answer to that. Deer meat is aged to tenderize the meat, much like beef. Younger deer do not need as much time to age as older animals. In addition, knowing how old the deer is may add to the pleasure of the hunt.

Whatever the reason for wanting to know the age of the deer, age determination can be done by examining the teeth. This technique is based on replacement and wear of the teeth in the deer's lower jaw and is accurate enough to judge a deer's age to within one year.

To get a good look at the lower jaw teeth, it is necessary to cut the skin on one or both sides of the cheek and force the jaw open. Those who plan to have the deer head mounted should refrain from this and should ask the taxidermist to return the lower jaw.

Biologist Ed Guljas examines a lower deer jaw at the Crosley Fish and Wildlife Area.

Figure #1. Cheek side of lower left jaw.

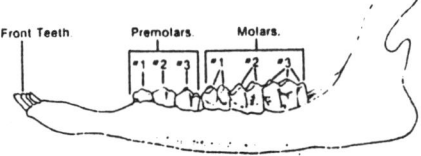

Figure #2. First and second set of premolars showing three-crowned third premolar of the first set and the two-crowned premolar of the second set.

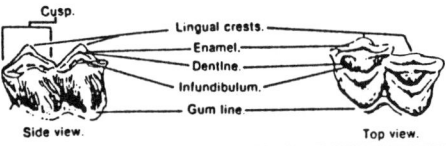

Figure #3. Parts of a molar.

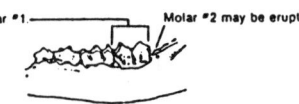

Figure #4. Fawn jaw teeth.

Figure #5. Yearling jaw teeth.

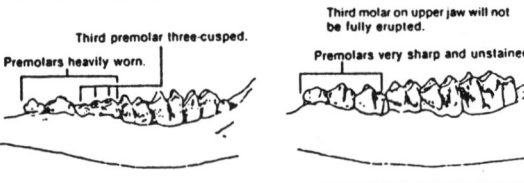

Of course, when using the teeth to determine a deer's age, it is important to know which teeth to look at and which parts of the teeth to examine. The teeth to look for are the premolars and molars of the lower jaw. The wear and replacement of these teeth will reveal the age of the deer. (Figure 1)

Premolars: Deer grow two sets of these. The first set, or baby teeth, will appear in fawns, and adults up to 1½ years old. At that age, a second, permanent set will replace the first. The two sets of premolars have one distinct difference: the third premolar of the baby teeth has three crowns, while the third premolar in the permanent set has only two. (Figure 2)

Molars: The molars are permanent teeth, but all three are not fully grown in until after 1½ years of age. These teeth wear at a predictable rate after the deer is 1½, and age can be determined by looking at these parts of the molars: the cusp or crown; the buccal or "cheek side" crest; the lingual or "tongue side" crest'; the enamel; the dentine; the infundibulum or space between the buccal and lingual crest; and the gum line. (Figure 3)

Another important point to remember when aging an Indiana deer is that almost all are born in May or June. This means that by the time a hunter is aging his deer in the fall, the deer has lived through at least one summer. For that reason, ages are given in half-year increments: ½, 1½, 2½, etc.

The youngest deer most likely to be encountered by a hunter will already be about six months old. Look for the set of temporary premolars, with the third premolar having three cusps. The first molar will be in place with possibly the second starting to come in. The third molar won't be seen. (Figure 4)

Deer that are 1½ years old may or may not have replaced their baby teeth with permanent premolars. But they will have all three molars in place. If they still have their temporary premolars, the teeth will be heavily worn. If the permanent premolars have come in, with the distinctive, two-cusped third molar, they will usually be very sharp and white. Some deer that are 1½ years old will have some staining on their permanent premolars. If this is the case, it would be easy to confuse them with 2½-year-old deer. To double check, look at the upper jaw (this is the only time that it's necessary to do so). If the third molar in the upper jaw has not completely come in, the deer is 1½ years old. (Figure 5)

If a deer has his permanent premolars, and these teeth are stained as dark as the molars, and if all teeth are completely in, it is time to check wearing of the teeth. Deer that are 2½ years old will have sharp lingual crests (six of them, two on each molar). These crests will be well above a very narrow dentine line. There will be wear on the first molar, but the lingual crests will still be sharp and the dentine line narrow. The last cusp on the third molar will be worn slightly, but little wear will be apparent on the premolars. (Figure 6)

The first molar on a 3½-year-old deer will have blunt lingual crests, and the dentine lines on the first and second molars will be wider than the enamel. Check the last cusp on the third molar. On a 3½-year-old deer, this will be flattened with a slightly concave top. The premolars will still be sharp, with little wear on the first two and moderate wear on the third. (Figure 7)

The lingual crests on the first molar of a 4½-year-old deer will be worn considerably, and the dentine will be about twice as wide as the enamel. The lingual crests on the second molar will be blunt, with the dentine line wider than the enamel. The last cusp of the third molar will slope toward the cheek side. The second and third premolars of a 4½-year-old deer will show moderate wear. (Figure 8)

A good way to tell a deer that is 5½ years old is to look at the first cusp on the first molar. A deer this age will show cupping of the first cusp, or in other words, the separation between the lingual and buccal crests will be worn away. On the second molar, the lingual crests will be very blunt and the dentine lines twice as wide as the enamel. The second and third premolars will show considerable wear. (Figure 9)

If both cusps on the first molar are cupped, chances are the deer is 6½ years old. Check the lingual crests on the second molar. On 6½-year-old deer, these will be worn away, and there will be only

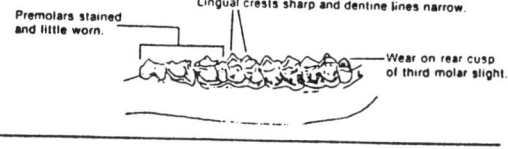

Figure #6. 2½ year jaw teeth.

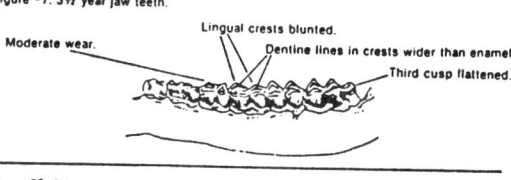

Figure #7. 3½ year jaw teeth.

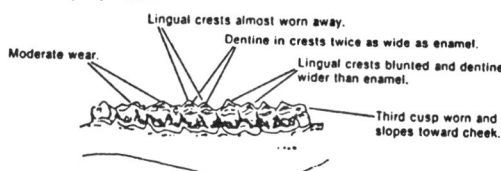

Figure #8. 4½ year jaw teeth.

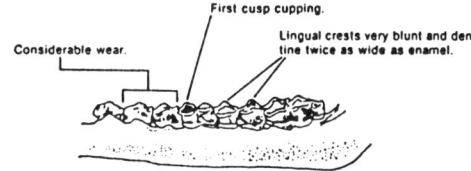

Figure #9. 5½ year jaw teeth.

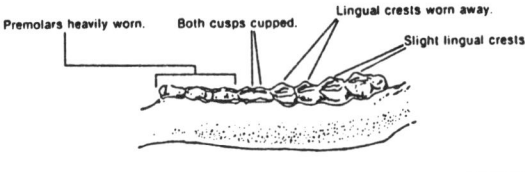

Figure #10. 6½ year jaw teeth.
Premolars heavily worn. Both cusps cupped. Lingual crests worn away. Slight lingual crests.

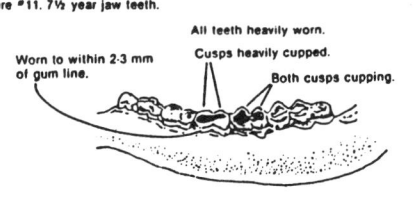

Figure #11. 7½ year jaw teeth.
Worn to within 2-3 mm of gum line. All teeth heavily worn. Cusps heavily cupped. Both cusps cupping.

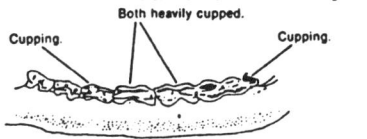

Figure #12. 8½ to 9½ year jaw teeth.
Cupping. All teeth worn to within 2-3 mm of gum line. Both heavily cupped. Cupping.

a slight lingual crest on the third molar. All premolars will be heavily worn. (Figure 10)

The first molar will be cupped and the second molar starting to cup on 7½-year-old deer. All teeth will be heavily worn, and the first molar will be worn to within 2 or 3 millimeters of the gum line on the cheek side. (Figure 11) On 8½- and 9½-year-old deer, all the teeth will be very heavily worn. The cusps on the first and second molars will be heavily cupped, and the third molar will be cupping. The third premolar will also be cupping, and all the premolars will be very heavily worn. All the premolars and molars will be worn to within 2 or 3 millimeters of the gum line on the cheek side. (Figure 12)

Deer that are 10½ years old or older show all teeth cupped, including the premolars. In 10½-year-old deer, the first molar will be worn down to or below the gum line on the cheek side. Past this age, the other teeth will begin to be worn below the gum line. Very few deer in this age group will be encountered, even though deer can survive to 16 years of age. Potential life expectancy is seldom reached for any species in the wild.

It should not be too difficult to place deer in one of the age groups described if the jaw teeth are examined carefully. But, as with almost every rule, there are exceptions. Some adult deer lack certain teeth, and some show more wear on one side of the mouth than on the other. In such a case, it's possible to have a difference of one year between the two sides. When this happens, the examiner should check both sides carefully and come up with a happy medium.

Some deer display characteristics of a certain age class in most, but not all teeth. That's why more than just one characteristic should always be considered.

This method of aging deer will take almost all the guesswork out of determining the age of the deer. Although it won't work in areas of the country where sandy conditions cause more rapid wearing of the teeth, it should provide Indiana hunters with a reliable technique.

Ed Guljas is a district wildlife biologist for a 10-county area in southeastern Indiana. He has been with the DNR for 12 years and has aged hundreds of deer with this method.

WHITE-TAILED DEER WEIGHT FORMULA

Take measurement of chest around heart, just behind front foreleg.
Chest measurement x 5.6037 - 94.0982 = Live Weight.
Live Weight x .78 = Field Weight.
Field Weight ÷ 2 = Edible Meat.

Chest	Live Weight	Field Weight	Meat	Chest	Live Weight	Field Weight	Meat	Chest	Live Weight	Field Weight	Meat
25	46	36	18	41	136	106	53	57	225	176	88
26	52	40	20	42	141	110	55	58	231	180	90
27	57	45	22	43	147	115	57	59	237	184	92
28	63	49	24	44	152	119	59	60	242	189	94
29	68	53	27	45	158	123	62	61	248	193	97
30	74	58	29	46	164	128	64	62	253	198	99
31	80	62	31	47	169	132	66	63	259	202	101
32	85	66	33	48	175	136	68	64	265	206	103
33	91	71	35	49	180	141	70	65	270	211	105
34	96	75	38	50	186	145	73	66	276	215	108
35	102	80	40	51	192	150	75	67	281	219	110
36	108	84	42	52	197	154	77	68	287	224	112
37	113	88	44	53	203	158	79	69	293	228	114
38	119	93	46	54	209	163	81	70	298	233	116
39	124	97	49	55	214	167	84	71	304	237	118
40	130	101	51	56	220	171	86	72	309	241	121

The following table from Gerald J. Grantz' Home Book of Taxidermy and Tanning should aid you in determining the leather yields of the Whitetail deer:

DRESSED DEER WEIGHT	HIDE SIZE	APPROXIMATE YIELD
90—130 lbs.	Small	6—8 sq. ft.
130—175 lbs.	Medium	9—11 sq. ft.
175—200 lbs.	Large	12—15 sq. ft.
Over 200 lbs.	Extra-Large	16—18 sq. ft.

One average-size deerskin yields enough leather for 3 pairs of gloves.
Moccasins require about 3 sq. ft.
Jackets & coats require 30 to 40 sq. ft.
Handbags require 4 to 6 sq. ft.
Purses, wallets, key cases, etc., are made from remaining scrap leather.

Chart reprinted from the Deer and Deer Hunting - Log Book, P.O. Box 1117, Appleton, Wisconsin, 54912

WINCHESTER® CENTERFIRE PISTOL/REVOLVER AMMUNITION

"WINCHESTER is a trademark of Olin Corporation and is used by permission. Neither the author nor the publisher are sponsored by or associated with Olin."

	Cartridge	Symbol	Bullet Wt. Grs.	Type	Velocity (fps) Muzzle	50 Yds.	100 Yds.	Energy (ft-lbs.) Muzzle	50 Yds.	100 Yds.	Mid Range Traj. (in.) 50 Yds.	100 Yds.	Barrel Length Inches
	25 Automatic	X25AXP	45	Expanding Point**	815	729	655	66	53	42	1.8	7.7	2
	25 Automatic	X25AP	50	Full Metal Jacket	760	707	659	64	56	48	2.0	8.7	2
	30 Luger (7.65mm)	X30LP	93	Full Metal Jacket	1220	1110	1040	305	255	225	0.9	3.5	4-1/2
	30 Carbine #	X30M1	110	Hollow Soft Point	1790	1601	1430	783	626	500	0.4	1.7	10
	32 Smith & Wesson	X32SWP	85	Lead-Round Nose	680	645	610	90	81	73	2.5	10.5	4
	32 Smith & Wesson Long	X32SWLP	98	Lead-Round Nose	705	670	635	115	98	88	2.3	10.5	4
	32 Short Colt	X32SCP	80	Lead-Round Nose	745	665	590	100	79	62	2.2	9.9	4
	32 Automatic	X32ASHP	60	Silvertip* Hollow Point	970	895	835	125	107	93	1.3	5.4	4
	32 Automatic	X32AP	71	Full Metal Jacket	905	855	810	129	115	97	1.4	5.8	4
	38 Smith & Wesson	X38SWP	145	Lead-Round Nose	685	650	620	150	135	125	2.4	10.0	4
	380 Automatic	X380ASHP	85	Silvertip Hollow Point	1000	921	860	189	160	140	1.2	5.1	3-3/4
	380 Automatic	X380AP	95	Full Metal Jacket	955	865	785	190	160	130	1.4	5.9	3-3/4
	38 Special	X38S9HP	110	Silvertip Hollow Point	945	894	850	218	195	176	1.3	5.4	4V
	38 Special Super Unleaded™	X38SU	130	Full Metal Jacket-Encapsulated	775	743	712	173	159	146	1.9	7.9	4V
New	38 Special Super Match*	X38SMRP	148	Lead-Wad Cutter	710	634	566	166	132	105	2.4	10.8	4V
	38 Special	X38S1P	158	Lead-Round Nose	755	723	693	200	183	168	2.0	8.3	4V
	38 Special	X38WCPSV	158	Lead-Semi Wad Cutter	755	721	689	200	182	167	2.0	8.4	4V
	38 Special + P	X38SSHP	95	Silvertip Hollow Point	1100	1002	932	255	212	183	1.0	4.3	4V
	38 Special + P	X38S6PH	110	Jacketed Hollow Point	995	926	871	242	210	185	1.2	5.1	4V
	38 Special + P‡	X38S7PH	125	Jacketed Hollow Point	945	898	858	248	224	204	1.3	5.4	4V
	38 Special Subsonic* + P	X38S8HP	125	Silvertip Hollow Point	945	898	858	248	224	204	1.3	5.4	4V
	38 Special Subsonic* + P	X38SUB38S	147	Jacketed Hollow Point	860	830	802	241	225	210	1.5	6.3	4V
	38 Special + P	X38SPD	158	Lead-Semi Wad Cutter Hollow Point	890	855	823	278	257	238	1.4	6.0	4V
	38 Special + P	X38WCP	158	Lead-Semi Wad Cutter	890	855	823	278	257	238	1.4	6.0	4V
New	9mm Luger Super Unleaded	X9MASU	115	Full Metal Jacket-Encapsulated	1155	1047	971	341	280	241	0.9	3.9	4
	9mm Luger	X9LP	115	Full Metal Jacket	1155	1047	971	341	280	241	0.9	3.9	4
	9mm Luger	X9MMSHP	115	Silvertip Hollow Point	1225	1095	1007	383	306	259	0.8	3.6	4
	9mm Luger Subsonic	X9LSUBMM	147	Jacketed Hollow Point	990	945	907	320	292	268	1.2	4.9	4
	9mm Luger	X9MMST147	147	Silvertip Hollow Point	1010	962	921	320	292	277	1.1	4.7	4
	9mm Luger Super Match	X9MMTCM	147	Full Metal Jacket-Truncated Cone-Match	990	945	907	320	292	268	1.2	4.8	4
	38 Super Automatic + P	X38ASHP	125	Silvertip Hollow Point	1240	1130	1050	427	354	306	0.8	3.4	5

Cartridge	Symbol	Bullet Wt. Grs.	Bullet Style	Muzzle	50 Yds.	100 Yds.	Muzzle	50 Yds.	100 Yds.	50 Yds.	100 Yds.	Barrel Length
38 Super Automatic + P	X38A1P	130	Full Metal Jacket	1215		1017	426		298	0.8	3.6	5
357 Magnum #	X3573P	110	Jacketed Hollow Point	1295	1095	975	410	292	232	0.8	3.5	4V
357 Magnum #	X3576P	125	Jacketed Hollow Point	1450	1240	1090	583	427	330	0.6	2.8	4V
357 Magnum #	X357SHP	145	Silvertip Hollow Point	1290	1155	1060	535	428	361	0.8	3.5	4V
357 Magnum	X3571P	158	Lead-Semi Wad Cutter**	1235	1104	1015	535	428	361	0.8	3.5	4V
357 Magnum	X3574P	158	Jacketed Soft Point	1235	1104	1015	535	428	361	0.8	3.5	4V
357 Magnum	X357SP	158	Silvertip Hollow Point	1235	1104	1015	535	428	361	0.8	3.5	4V
40 Smith & Wesson	X40SWSTHP	155	Silvertip Hollow Point	1205	1096	1018	500	414	357	0.8	3.6	4
40 Smith & Wesson Super Match	X40SWTCM	155	Full Metal Jacket-Truncated Cone-Match	1125	1046	986	436	377	335	0.9	3.9	4
New 40 Smith & Wesson Super Unleaded	X40SWSU	180	Full Metal Jacket-Encapsulated	990	933	886	392	348	314	1.2	5.0	4
40 Smith & Wesson Subsonic	XSUB40SW	180	Jacketed Hollow Point	1010	954	909	408	364	330	1.1	4.8	4
10mm Automatic Super Match	X10MMTCM	155	Full Metal Jacket-Truncated Cone-Match	1125	1046	986	436	377	335	0.9	3.9	5
10mm Automatic	X10MMSTHP	175	Silvertip Hollow Point	1290	1141	1037	646	506	418	0.7	3.3	5-1/2
10mm Automatic Subsonic	XSUB10MM	180	Jacketed Hollow Point	980	936	891	390	350	317	1.2	4.9	5
41 Remington Magnum #	X41MSTHP2	175	Silvertip Hollow Point	1250	1120	1029	607	488	412	0.8	3.4	4V
41 Remington Magnum #	X41MHP2	210	Jacketed Hollow Point	1300	1162	1062	788	630	526	0.7	3.2	4V
44 Smith & Wesson Special #	X44STHP2	200	Silvertip Hollow Point	900	860	822	360	328	300	1.4	5.9	6-1/2
44 Smith & Wesson Special	X44SP	246	Lead-Round Nose	755	725	695	310	285	265	2.0	8.3	6-1/2
44 Remington Magnum	X44MSTHP2	210	Silvertip Hollow Point	1250	1106	1010	729	570	475	0.8	3.5	4V
44 Remington Magnum	X44MHSP2	240	Hollow Soft Point	1180	1081	1010	741	623	543	0.9	3.7	4V
45 Automatic	X45ASHP2	185	Silvertip Hollow Point	1000	938	888	411	362	324	1.2	4.9	5
45 Automatic Super Match	X45AWCP	185	Full Metal Jacket-Semi Wad Cutter	770	707	650	244	205	174	2.0	8.7	5
45 Automatic Subsonic	XSUB45A	220	Jacketed Hollow Point	925	880	840	437	398	361	1.3	5.6	5
45 Automatic	X45A1P2	230	Full Metal Jacket	835	800	767	356	326	300	1.6	6.8	5
45 Colt #	X45CSHP2	225	Silvertip Hollow Point	920	877	839	423	384	352	1.4	5.6	5-1/2
45 Colt	X45CP2	255	Lead-Round Nose	860	820	780	420	380	345	1.5	6.1	5-1/2
45 Winchester Magnum # (Not for Arms Chambered for Standard 45 Automatic)	X45WM2	230	Full Metal Jacket	1400	1232	1107	1001	775	636	0.6	2.8	5
New 45 Winchester Magnum # (Not for Arms Chambered for Standard 45 Automatic)	X45WMA	260	Jacketed Soft Point	—	—	—	Under Development	—	—	—	—	—

+P Ammunition with (+P) on the case head stamp is loaded to higher pressure. Use only in firearms designated for this cartridge and so recommended by the gun manufacturer.

V-Data is based on velocity obtained from 4" vented test barrels for revolver cartridges (38 Special, 357 Magnum, 41 Rem. Mag. and 44 Rem. Mag.)
Specifications are nominal. Test barrels are used to determine ballistics figures. Individual firearms may differ from test barrel statistics.

Specifications subject to change without notice.

**"Lubaloy® Coated
#For use only in 38 Super Automatic Pistols.
#Acceptable for use in rifles also.

WINCHESTER® CENTERFIRE RIFLE AMMUNITION

Game Selector
V-Varmint
D-Deer
O/P-Open or Plains
M-Medium Game
L-Large Game
XL-Extra Large Game

Acceptable for use in pistols and revolvers also
Bold type indicates Supreme® product line

Cartridge	Symbol	Selector Guide	Guide Number	Wt. Grs.	Bullet Type	Barrel Length (In.)	Velocity in Feet Per Second (fps)					
							Muzzle	100	200	300	400	500
218 Bee	X218B	V	1	46	Hollow Point	24	2760	2102	1550	1155	961	850
22 Hornet	X22H1	V	1	45	Soft Point	24	2690	2042	1502	1128	948	840
22 Hornet	X22H2	V	1	46	Hollow Point	24	2690	2042	1502	1128	948	841
22-250 Remington	S22250	V	1	52	Hollow Point Boattail	24	3750	3268	2835	2442	2082	1755
22-250 Remington	X222501	V	1	55	Pointed Soft Point	24	3680	3137	2656	2222	1832	1493
222 Remington	X222R	V	1	50	Pointed Soft Point	24	3140	2602	2123	1700	1350	1107
222 Remington	X222R1	V	1	55	Full Metal Jacket	24	3020	2675	2355	2057	1783	1537
223 Remington	X223RH	V	1	53	Hollow Point	24	3330	2882	2477	2106	1770	1475
223 Remington	X223R	V	1	55	Pointed Soft Point	24	3240	2747	2304	1905	1554	1270
223 Remington	X223R1	V	1	55	Full Metal Jacket	24	3240	2877	2543	2232	1943	1679
223 Remington	X223R2	D	2	64	Power-Point®	24	3020	2621	2256	1920	1619	1362
223 Remington Match	S223M*	–	M	69	Hollow Point Boattail	24	3060	2740	2442	2164	1904	1665
225 Winchester	X2251	V	1	55	Pointed Soft Point	24	3570	3066	2616	2208	1838	1514
243 Winchester	X2431	V	1	80	Pointed Soft Point	24	3350	2955	2593	2259	1951	1670
243 Winchester	X2432	D,O/P	2	100	Power-Point	24	2960	2697	2449	2215	1993	1786
243 Winchester	S243	D,O/P	2	100	Soft Point Boattail	24	2960	2712	2477	2254	2042	1843
6mm Remington	X6MMR1	V	1	80	Pointed Soft Point	24	3470	3064	2694	2352	2036	1747
6mm Remington	X6MMR2	D,O/P	2	100	Power-Point	24	3100	2829	2573	2332	2104	1889
25-06 Remington	X25061	V	1	90	Positive Expanding Point	24	3440	3043	2680	2344	2034	1749
25-06 Remington	X25062	D,O/P	2	120	Positive Expanding Point	24	2990	2730	2484	2252	2032	1825
25-20 Winchester #	X25202	V	1	86	Soft Point	24	1460	1194	1030	931	858	798
25-35 Winchester	X2535	D	2	117	Soft Point	24	2230	1866	1545	1282	1097	984
250 Savage	X2503	D,O/P	2	100	Silvertip	24	2820	2467	2140	1839	1569	1339
257 Roberts + P	X257P3	D,O/P	2	117	Power-Point	24	2780	2411	2071	1761	1488	1263
264 Winchester Mag.	X2642	D,O/P	2	140	Power-Point	24	3030	2782	2548	2326	2114	1914
New 6.5 x 55 Swedish	X6555	D,O/P	2	140	Soft Point	–	–	–	–	–	–	–
270 Winchester	X2701	V	1	100	Pointed Soft Point	24	3430	3021	2649	2305	1988	1699
270 Winchester	X2705	D,O/P	2	130	Power-Point	24	3060	2802	2559	2329	2110	1904
270 Winchester	X2703	D,O/P	2	130	Silvertip	24	3060	2776	2510	2259	2022	1801
270 Winchester	S270	D,O/P	2	140	Silvertip Boattail	24	2960	2753	2554	2365	2183	2009
New 270 Winchester Fail Safe®	S270X	–	–	–	–	–	–	–	–	–	–	–
270 Winchester	X2704	D,M	3	150	Power-Point	24	2850	2585	2336	2100	1879	1673
280 Remington	X280R	D,O/P	2	140	Power-Point	24	3050	2705	2428	2167	1924	1698
280 Remington	S280R	D,O/P	2	160	Silvertip Boattail	24	2840	2637	2442	2256	2078	1909
284 Winchester	X2842	D,O/P,M	3	150	Power-Point	24	2860	2595	2344	2108	1886	1680
7mm Mauser (7x57)	X7MM1	D	2	145	Power-Point	24	2660	2413	2180	1959	1751	1564
7mm Remington Mag.	S7MAG	D,O/P	2	139	Soft Point Boattail	24	3165	2935	2717	2509	2311	2121
7mm Remington Mag.	X7MMR1	D,O/P,M	2	150	Power-Point	24	3110	2830	2568	2320	2085	1866
7mm Remington Mag.	S7MAGA	D,O/P,M,L	3	160	Silvertip Boattail	24	2950	2745	2550	2363	2184	2012
New 7mm Remington Mag. Fail Safe®	S7MAGX	–	–	–	–	–	–	–	–	–	–	–
7mm Remington Mag.	X7MMR2	D,O/P,M	3	175	Power-Point	24	2860	2645	2440	2244	2057	1879
7.62 x 39mm Russian	X76239	D,V	2	123	Soft Point	20	2365	2033	1731	1465	1248	1093
30 Carbine #	X30M1	V	1	110	Hollow Soft Point	20	1990	1567	1236	1035	923	842
30-30 Winchester	S3030W150	D	2	150	Silvertip	24	2390	2018	1684	1398	1177	1036
30-30 Winchester	X30301	D	2	150	Hollow Point	24	2390	2018	1684	1398	1177	1036
30-30 Winchester	X30306	D	2	150	Power-Point	24	2390	2018	1684	1398	1177	1036
30-30 Winchester	X30302	D	2	150	Silvertip	24	2390	2018	1684	1398	1177	1036

CXP Class	Examples
1	Prairie dog, coyote, woodchuck
2	Antelope, deer, black bear
3	Elk, moose
3D	All game in category 3 plus large dangerous game (i.e. Kodiak bear)
4	Cape Buffalo, elephant
M	Match

*Intended for use in fast twist barrels (e.g., 1 in 7 to 1 in 9).
Slower twist barrels may not sufficiently stabilize bullet.

Energy in Foot Pounds (ft-lbs.)						Trajectory, Short Range Yards						Trajectory, Long Range Yards					
Muzzle	100	200	300	400	500	50	100	150	200	250	300	100	150	200	250	300	400	500
778	451	245	136	94	74	0.3	0	-2.3	-7.2	-15.8	-29.4	1.5	0	-4.2	-12.0	-24.8	-71.4	-155.6
723	417	225	127	90	70	0.3	0	-2.4	-7.7	-16.9	-31.5	1.6	0	-4.5	-12.6	-26.4	-75.6	-163.4
739	426	230	130	92	72	0.3	0	-2.4	-7.7	-16.9	-31.3	1.6	0	-4.5	-12.6	-26.4	-75.5	-163.3
1624	1233	928	689	501	356	0.1	0	-0.7	-2.4	-5.1	-9.1	1.2	1.1	0	-2.1	-5.5	-16.9	-36.3
1654	1201	861	603	410	272	0.2	0.5	0	-1.6	-4.4	-8.7	2.3	2.6	1.9	0	-3.4	-15.9	-38.9
1094	752	500	321	202	136	0.5	0.9	0	-2.5	-6.9	-13.7	2.2	1.9	0	-3.8	-10.0	-32.3	-73.6
1114	874	677	517	388	288	0.5	0.9	0	-2.2	-6.1	-11.7	2.0	1.7	0	-3.3	-8.3	-24.9	-52.5
1305	978	722	522	369	256	0.3	0.7	0	-1.9	-5.3	-10.3	1.7	1.4	0	-2.9	-7.4	-22.7	-49.1
1282	921	648	443	295	197	0.4	0.8	0	-2.2	-6.0	-11.8	1.9	1.6	0	-3.3	-8.5	-26.7	-59.6
1282	1011	790	608	461	344	0.4	0.7	0	-1.9	-5.1	-9.9	1.7	1.4	0	-2.8	-7.1	-21.2	-44.6
1296	977	723	524	373	264	0.6	0.9	0	-2.4	-6.5	-12.5	2.1	1.8	0	-3.5	-9.0	-27.4	-59.6
1435	1151	914	717	555	425	-0.2	0	-0.9	-3.1	-6.8	-12.1	1.6	1.4	0	-2.9	-7.4	-22.3	-46.7
1556	1148	836	595	412	280	0.2	0.6	0	-1.7	-4.6	-9.0	2.4	2.8	2.0	0	-3.5	-16.3	-39.5
1993	1551	1194	906	676	495	0.3	0.7	0	-1.8	-4.9	-9.4	2.6	2.9	2.1	0	-3.6	-16.2	-37.9
1945	1615	1332	1089	882	708	0.5	0.9	0	-2.2	-5.8	-11.0	1.9	1.6	0	-3.1	-7.8	-22.6	-46.3
1946	1633	1363	1128	926	754	0.1	0	-1.3	-3.8	-7.8	-13.3	1.9	1.6	0	-3.0	-7.6	-22.0	-44.8
2139	1667	1289	982	736	542	0.3	0.6	0	-1.6	-4.5	-8.7	2.4	2.7	1.9	0	-3.3	-14.9	-35.0
2133	1777	1470	1207	983	792	0.4	0.8	0	-1.9	-5.2	-9.9	1.7	1.5	0	-2.8	-7.0	-20.4	-41.7
2364	1850	1435	1098	827	611	0.3	0.6	0	-1.7	-4.5	-8.8	2.4	2.7	2.0	0	-3.4	-15.0	-35.2
2382	1985	1644	1351	1100	887	0.5	0.8	0	-2.1	-5.6	-10.7	1.9	1.6	0	-3.0	-7.5	-22.0	-44.8
407	272	203	165	141	122	0	-4.1	-14.4	-31.8	-57.3	-92.0	0	-8.2	-23.5	-47.0	-79.8	-175.9	-319.4
1292	904	620	427	313	252	0.6	0	-3.1	-9.2	-19.0	-33.1	2.1	0	-5.1	-13.8	-27.0	-70.1	-142.0
1765	1351	1017	751	547	398	0.2	0	-1.6	-4.9	-10.0	-17.4	2.4	2.0	0	-3.9	-10.1	-30.5	-65.2
2009	1511	1115	806	576	415	0.8	1.1	0	-2.9	-7.8	-15.1	2.6	2.2	0	-4.2	-10.8	-33.0	-70.0
2854	2406	2018	1682	1389	1139	0.5	0.8	0	-2.0	-5.4	-10.2	1.8	1.5	0	-2.9	-7.2	-20.8	-42.2
Under Development																		
2612	2027	1557	1179	877	641	0.3	0.6	0	-1.7	-4.6	-9.0	2.5	2.8	2.0	0	-3.4	-15.5	-36.4
2702	2267	1890	1565	1285	1046	0.4	0.8	0	-2.0	-5.3	-10.1	1.8	1.5	0	-2.8	-7.1	-20.6	-42.0
2702	2225	1818	1472	1180	936	0.5	0.8	0	-2.0	-5.5	-10.4	1.8	1.5	0	-2.9	-7.4	-21.6	-44.3
2724	2356	2020	1739	1482	1256	0.1	0	-1.2	-3.7	-7.5	-12.7	1.8	1.5	0	-2.9	-7.2	-20.6	-41.3
Under Development						-	-	-	-	-	-	-	-	-	-	-	-	-
2705	2226	1817	1468	1175	932	0.6	1.0	0	-2.4	-6.4	-12.2	2.2	1.8	0	-3.4	-8.6	-25.0	-51.4
2799	2274	1833	1461	1151	897	0.5	0.8	0	-2.2	-5.8	-11.1	1.9	1.6	0	-3.1	-7.8	-23.1	-47.8
2866	2471	2120	1809	1535	1295	0.1	0	-1.4	-4.1	-8.3	-14.0	2.1	1.7	0	-3.2	-7.9	-22.6	-45.4
2724	2243	1830	1480	1185	940	0.6	1.0	0	-2.4	-6.3	-12.1	2.1	1.8	0	-3.4	-8.5	-24.8	-51.0
2279	1875	1530	1236	990	788	0.2	0	-1.7	-5.1	-10.3	-17.5	1.1	0	-2.8	-7.4	-14.1	-34.4	-66.1
3093	2588	2279	1944	1648	1389	0.1	0	-1.0	-3.2	-6.5	-11.1	1.6	1.3	0	-2.5	-6.3	-18.3	-36.6
3221	2667	2196	1792	1448	1160	0.4	0.8	0	-1.9	-5.2	-9.9	1.7	1.5	0	-2.8	-7.0	-20.5	-42.1
3093	2679	2311	1984	1694	1439	0.1	0	-1.2	-3.7	-7.5	-12.8	1.9	1.5	0	-2.9	-7.2	-20.6	-41.4
Under Development						-	-	-	-	-	-	-	-	-	-	-	-	-
3178	2718	2313	1956	1644	1372	0.6	0.9	0	-2.3	-6.0	-11.3	2.0	1.7	0	-3.2	-7.9	-22.7	-45.8
1527	1129	818	586	425	327	0.5	0	-2.6	-7.6	-15.4	-26.7	3.8	3.1	0	-6.0	-15.4	-46.3	-98.4
967	600	373	262	208	173	0.9	0	-4.5	-13.5	-28.3	-49.9	0	-4.5	-13.5	-28.3	-49.9	-118.6	-228.2
1902	1356	944	651	461	357	0.5	0	-2.6	-7.7	-16.0	-27.9	3.9	3.2	0	-6.2	-16.1	-49.4	-105.2
1902	1356	944	651	461	357	0.5	0	-2.6	-7.7	-16.0	-27.9	1.7	0	-4.3	-11.6	-22.7	-59.1	-120.5
1902	1356	944	651	461	357	0.5	0	-2.6	-7.7	-16.0	-27.9	1.7	0	-4.3	-11.6	-22.7	-59.1	-120.5
1902	1356	944	651	461	357	0.5	0	-2.6	-7.7	-16.0	-27.9	1.7	0	-4.3	-11.6	-22.7	-59.1	-120.5

Cartridge	Symbol			Wt. (grs)	Bullet Type	Bbl. (in)	Muzzle	100 yd	200 yd	300 yd	400 yd	500 yd
30-30 Winchester	X30303	D	2	170	Power-Point	24	2200	1895	1619	1381	1191	1061
30-30 Winchester	X30304	D	2	170	Silvertip	24	2200	1895	1619	1381	1191	1061
30-06 Springfield	X30062	V	1	125	Pointed Soft Point	24	3140	2780	2447	2138	1853	1595
30-06 Springfield	X30061	D,O/P	2	150	Power-Point	24	2920	2580	2265	1972	1704	1466
30-06 Springfield	X30063	D,O/P	2	150	Silvertip	24	2910	2617	2342	2083	1843	1622
30-06 Springfield	**S3006**	D,O/P,M	2	165	Silvertip Boattail	24	**2800**	**2597**	**2402**	**2216**	**2038**	**1869**
30-06 Springfield	X30065	D,O/P,M	2	165	Soft Point	24	2800	2573	2357	2151	1956	1772
30-06 Springfield	**S3006A**	D,O/P,M,L	3	180	Silvertip Boattail	24	**2700**	**2503**	**2314**	**2133**	**1960**	**1797**
30-06 Springfield	**S3006X**	D,O/P,M,L	3	180	Fail Safe	24	**2700**	**2486**	**2283**	**2089**	**1904**	**1731**
Fail Safe												
30-06 Springfield	X30064	D,O/P,M	2	180	Power-Point	24	2700	2348	2023	1727	1466	1251
30-06 Springfield	X30066	D,O/P,M,L	3	180	Silvertip	24	2700	2469	2250	2042	1846	1663
30-06 Springfield	X30069	M,L		220	Silvertip	24	2410	2192	1985	1791	1611	1448
30-40 Krag	X30401	D	2	180	Power-Point	24	2430	2099	1795	1525	1298	1128
300 Winchester Mag.	X30WM1	D,O/P	2	150	Power-Point	24	3290	2951	2636	2342	2068	1813
300 Winchester Mag.	**S300WX**	M,L	3D	180	Fail Safe	24	**2960**	**2732**	**2514**	**2307**	**2110**	**1923**
Fail Safe												
300 Winchester Mag.	X30WM2	O/P,M,L	3	180	Power-Point	24	2960	2745	2540	2344	2157	1979
300 Winchester Mag.	**S300W**	O/P,M,L	3D	190	Silvertip Boattail	24	**2885**	**2698**	**2519**	**2347**	**2181**	**2023**
300 Winchester Mag.	X30WM3	M,L,XL	3D	220	Silvertip	24	2680	2448	2228	2020	1823	1640
300 H&H Magnum	X300H2	D	3	180	Silvertip	24	2880	2640	2412	2196	1991	1798
300 Savage	X3001	D,O/P	2	150	Power-Point	24	2630	2311	2015	1743	1500	1295
300 Savage	X3003	D,O/P	2	150	Silvertip	24	2630	2354	2095	1853	1631	1434
300 Savage	X3004	D	2	180	Power-Point	24	2350	2025	1728	1467	1252	1098
303 Savage	X3032	D	2	190	Silvertip	24	1890	1612	1372	1183	1055	970
303 British	X30381	D	2	180	Silvertip	24	2460	2233	2018	1816	1629	1459
307 Winchester	X3076	D	2	180	Power-Point	24	2510	2179	1874	1599	1362	1177
308 Winchester	**S308W150**	D,O/P	2	150	Silvertip Boattail	24	**2820**	**2559**	**2312**	**2080**	**1861**	**1659**
308 Winchester	X3085	D,O/P	2	150	Power-Point	24	2820	2488	2179	1893	1633	1405
308 Winchester	X3082	D,O/P	2	150	Silvertip	24	2820	2533	2263	2009	1774	1560
308 Winchester Match	**S308M**	-	M	168	Hollow Point Boattail	24	**2680**	**2485**	**2297**	**2118**	**1948**	**1786**
308 Winchester	**S308W180**	D,O/P,M	3	180	Silvertip Boattail	24	**2610**	**2424**	**2245**	**2074**	**1911**	**1756**
308 Winchester	**S308X**	D,O/P,M,L	3	180	Fail Safe	24	**2620**	**2409**	**2207**	**2015**	**1834**	**1664**
Fail Safe												
308 Winchester	X3086	D,O/P,M	2	180	Power-Point	24	2620	2274	1955	1666	1414	1212
308 Winchester	X3083	M,L	3	180	Silvertip	24	2620	2393	2178	1974	1782	1604
32 Win Special	X32WS2	D	2	170	Power-Point	24	2250	1870	1537	1267	1082	971
32 Win Special	X32WS3	D	2	170	Silvertip	24	2250	1870	1537	1267	1082	971
32-20 Winchester	X32201	V	1	100	Lead	24	1210	1021	913	834	769	712
8mm Mauser (8 x 57)	X8MM	D	2	170	Power-Point	24	2360	1969	1622	1333	1123	997
338 Winchester Mag.	X3381	D,O/P,M	3	200	Power-Point	24	2960	2658	2375	2110	1862	1635
338 Winchester Mag.	X3383	M,L,XL	3D	225	Soft Point	24	2780	2572	2374	2184	2003	1832
338 Winchester Mag.	**S338XA**	M,L,XL	3D	230	Fail Safe	24	**2780**	**2573**	**2375**	**2186**	**2005**	**1834**
Fail Safe												
348 Winchester	Q3167	D,M	3	200	Silvertip	24	2520	2215	1931	1672	1443	1253
35 Remington	X35R1	D	2	200	Power-Point	24	2020	1646	1335	1114	985	901
356 Winchester	X3561	D,M	2	200	Power-Point	24	2460	2114	1797	1517	1284	1113
356 Winchester	X3563	M,L	3	250	Power-Point	24	2160	1911	1682	1476	1299	1158
357 Magnum	X357SP	V,D	2	158	Jacketed Soft Point	20	1830	1427	1138	960	883	809
358 Winchester	X3581	D,M	3	200	Silvertip	24	2490	2171	1876	1610	1379	1194
375 Winchester	X375W	D,M	2	200	Power-Point	24	2200	1841	1526	1268	1089	980
375 H&H Magnum	X375H1	M,L,XL	3D	270	Power-Point	24	2690	2420	2166	1928	1707	1507
375 H&H Magnum	X375H2	M,L,XL	3D	300	Silvertip	24	2530	2268	2022	1793	1583	1397
375 H&H Magnum	X375H3	XL		300	Full Metal Jacket	24	2530	2171	1843	1551	1307	1126
38-40 Winchester	X3840	D	2	180	Soft Point	24	1160	999	901	827	764	710
38-55 Winchester	X3855	D	2	255	Power-Point	24	1320	1190	1091	1018	963	917
44 Remington Magnum	X44MSTHP2	V,D	2	210	Silvertip Hollow Point	20	1580	1198	993	879	795	725
44 Remington Magnum	X44MHSP2	D	2	240	Hollow Soft Point	20	1760	1362	1094	953	861	789
44-40 Winchester	X4440	D	2	200	Soft Point	24	1190	1006	900	822	756	699
45-70 Government	X4570H	D,M	2	300	Jacketed Hollow Point	24	1880	1650	1425	1235	1105	1010
458 Winchester Magnum	X4580	XL	4	500	Full Metal Jacket	24	2040	1823	1623	1442	1287	1161
458 Winchester Magnum	X4581	L,XL	3D	510	Soft Point	24	2040	1770	1527	1319	1157	1046

1827	1355	989	720	535	425	0.6	0	-3.0	-8.9	-18.0	-31.1	2.0	0	-4.8	-13.0	-25.1	-63.6 -126.7
1827	1355	989	720	535	425	0.6	0	-3.0	-8.9	-18.0	-31.1	2.0	0	-4.8	-13.0	-25.1	-63.6 -126.7
2736	2145	1662	1269	953	706	0.4	0.8	0	-2.1	-5.6	-10.7	1.8	1.5	0	-3.0	-7.7	-23.0 -48.5
2839	2217	1708	1295	967	716	0.6	1.0	0	-2.4	-6.6	-12.7	2.2	1.8	0	-3.5	-9.0	-27.0 -57.1
2820	2281	1827	1445	1131	876	0.6	0.9	0	-2.3	-6.3	-12.0	2.1	1.8	0	-3.3	-8.5	-25.0 -51.8
2873	2421	2114	1799	1522	1280	0.1	0	-1.4	-4.3	-8.6	-14.6	2.1	1.8	0	-3.3	-8.2	-23.4 -47.0
2873	2426	2036	1696	1402	1151	0.7	1.0	0	-2.5	-6.5	-12.2	2.2	1.9	0	-3.6	-8.4	-24.4 -49.6
2914	2504	2148	1819	1536	1290	0.2	0	-1.6	-4.7	-9.4	-15.8	2.3	1.9	0	-3.5	-8.8	-25.3 -50.8
2914	2472	2083	1744	1450	1198	-0.1	0	-1.3	-4.1	-8.6	-14.9	2.1	1.8	0	-3.5	-8.7	-25.5 -51.8
2913	2203	1635	1192	859	625	0.2	0	-1.8	-5.5	-11.2	-19.5	2.7	2.3	0	-4.4	-11.3	-34.4 -73.7
2913	2436	2023	1666	1362	1105	0.2	0	-1.6	-4.8	-9.7	-16.5	2.4	2.0	0	-3.7	-9.3	-27.0 -54.9
2837	2347	1924	1567	1268	1024	0.4	0	-2.2	-6.4	-12.7	-21.6	1.5	0	-3.5	-9.1	-17.2	-41.8 -79.9
2360	1761	1288	929	673	508	0.4	0	-2.4	-7.1	-14.5	-25.0	1.6	0	-3.9	-10.5	-20.3	-51.7 -103.9
3605	2900	2314	1827	1424	1095	0.3	0.7	0	-1.8	-4.8	-9.3	2.6	2.9	2.1	0	-3.5	-15.4 -35.5
3503	2983	2528	2129	1788	1478	-0.2	0	-1.0	-3.2	-6.8	-11.8	1.6	1.4	0	-2.8	-7.1	-20.7 -42.1
3501	3011	2578	2196	1859	1565	0.5	0.8	0	-2.1	-5.5	-10.4	1.9	1.6	0	-2.9	-7.3	-20.9 -41.9
3512	3073	2679	2325	2009	1728	0.1	0	-1.3	-3.9	-7.8	-13.2	1.9	1.6	0	-3.0	-7.4	-21.1 -42.2
3508	2927	2424	1993	1623	1314	0.2	0	-1.7	-4.9	-9.9	-16.9	2.5	2.0	0	-3.8	-9.5	-27.5 -56.1
3315	2785	2325	1927	1584	1292	0.6	0.9	0	-2.3	-6.0	-11.5	2.1	1.7	0	-3.2	-8.0	-23.3 -47.4
2303	1779	1352	1012	749	558	0.3	0	-1.9	-5.7	-11.6	-19.9	2.8	2.3	0	-4.5	-11.5	-34.4 -73.0
2303	1845	1462	1143	886	685	0.3	0	-1.8	-5.4	-11.0	-18.8	2.7	2.2	0	-4.2	-10.7	-31.5 -65.5
2207	1639	1193	860	626	482	0.5	0	-2.6	-7.7	-15.6	-27.1	1.7	0	-4.2	-11.3	-21.9	-55.8 -112.0
1507	1096	794	591	469	397	1.0	0	-4.3	-12.6	-25.5	-43.7	2.9	0	-6.8	-18.3	-35.1	-88.2 -172.5
2418	1993	1627	1318	1060	851	0.3	0	-2.1	-6.1	-12.2	-20.8	1.4	0	-3.3	-8.8	-16.6	-40.4 -77.4
2519	1898	1404	1022	742	554	0.3	0	-2.2	-6.5	-13.3	-22.9	1.5	0	-3.6	-9.6	-18.6	-47.1 -93.7
2649	2182	1782	1441	1154	917	0.2	0	-1.5	-4.4	-9.0	-15.4	2.2	1.8	0	-3.5	-8.7	-25.5 -52.3
2648	2061	1581	1193	888	657	0.2	0	-1.6	-4.8	-9.8	-16.9	2.4	2.0	0	-3.8	-9.8	-29.3 -62.0
2648	2137	1705	1344	1048	810	0.2	0	-1.5	-4.5	-9.3	-15.9	2.3	1.9	0	-3.6	-9.1	-26.9 -55.7
2688	2303	1970	1674	1415	1190	-0.1	0	-1.3	-4.1	-8.6	-14.9	2.1	1.8	0	-3.4	-8.7	-25.1 -50.7
2723	2348	2015	1719	1459	1232	0.2	0	-1.7	-5.0	-10.1	-17.0	2.5	2.1	0	-3.8	-9.4	-26.9 -54.0
2744	2319	1947	1624	1344	1107	-0.1	0	-1.4	-4.5	-9.4	-16.2	2.3	1.9	0	-3.7	-9.4	-27.4 -55.7
2743	2066	1527	1109	799	587	0.3	0	-2.0	-5.9	-12.1	-20.9	2.9	2.4	0	-4.7	-12.1	-36.9 -79.1
2743	2288	1896	1557	1269	1028	0.2	0	-1.8	-5.2	-10.4	-17.7	2.6	2.1	0	-4.0	-9.9	-28.9 -58.8
1911	1320	892	606	442	356	0.6	0	-3.1	-9.2	-19.0	-33.2	2.0	0	-5.1	-13.8	-27.1	-70.9 -144.3
1911	1320	892	606	442	356	0.6	0	-3.1	-9.2	-19.0	-33.2	2.0	0	-5.1	-13.8	-27.1	-70.9 -144.3
325	231	185	154	131	113	0	-6.3	-20.9	-44.9	-79.3	-125.1	0	-11.5	-32.3	-63.6	-106.3	-230.3 -413.3
2102	1463	993	671	476	375	0.5	0	-2.7	-8.2	-17.0	-29.8	1.8	0	-4.5	-12.4	-24.3	-63.8 -130.7
3890	3137	2505	1977	1539	1187	0.5	0.9	0	-2.3	-6.1	-11.6	2.0	1.7	0	-3.3	-8.2	-24.3 -50.4
3862	3306	2816	2384	2005	1677	1.2	1.3	0	-2.7	-7.1	-12.9	2.7	2.1	0	-3.6	-9.4	-25.0 -49.9
3948	3382	2861	2441	2054	1719	-0.1	0	-1.2	-3.8	-7.9	-13.7	1.9	1.7	0	-3.2	-8.1	-23.4 -47.4
2820	2178	1656	1241	925	697	0.3	0	-2.1	-6.2	-12.7	-21.9	1.4	0	-3.4	-9.2	-17.7	-44.4 -87.9
1812	1203	791	551	431	360	0.9	0	-4.1	-12.1	-25.1	-43.9	2.7	0	-6.7	-18.3	-35.8	-92.8 -185.5
2688	1985	1434	1022	732	550	0.4	0	-2.3	-7.0	-14.3	-24.7	1.6	0	-3.8	-10.4	-20.1	-51.2 -102.3
2591	2028	1571	1210	937	745	0.6	0	-3.0	-8.7	-17.4	-30.0	2.0	0	-4.7	-12.4	-23.7	-58.4 -112.9
1175	715	454	337	274	229	0	-2.4	-9.1	-21.0	-39.2	-64.3	0	-5.5	-16.2	-33.1	-57.0	-128.3 -235.8
2753	2093	1563	1151	844	633	0.4	0	-2.2	-6.5	-13.3	-23.0	1.5	0	-3.6	-9.7	-18.6	-47.2 -94.1
2150	1506	1034	714	527	427	0.6	0	-3.2	-9.5	-19.5	-33.8	2.1	0	-5.2	-14.1	-27.4	-70.1 -138.1
4337	3510	2812	2228	1747	1361	0.2	0	-1.7	-5.1	-10.3	-17.6	2.5	2.1	0	-3.9	-10.0	-29.4 -60.7
4263	3426	2723	2141	1669	1300	0.3	0	-2.0	-5.9	-11.9	-20.3	2.9	2.4	0	-4.5	-11.5	-33.8 -70.1
4263	3139	2262	1602	1138	844	0.3	0	-2.2	-6.5	-13.5	-23.4	1.5	0	-3.6	-9.8	-19.1	-49.1 -99.5
538	399	324	273	233	201	0	-6.7	-22.2	-47.3	-83.2	-130.8	0	-12.1	-33.9	-66.4	-110.6	-238.3 -345.9
987	802	674	587	525	476	0	-4.7	-15.4	-32.7	-57.2	-89.3	0	-8.4	-23.4	-45.6	-75.2	-158.8 -277.4
1164	670	460	361	295	245	0	-3.7	-13.3	-29.8	-54.2	-87.3	0	-7.7	-22.4	-44.9	-76.1	-168.0 -305.8
1650	988	638	484	395	332	0	-2.7	-10.2	-23.6	-44.2	-73.3	0	-6.1	-18.1	-37.4	-65.1	-150.3 -282.5
629	449	360	300	254	217	0	-6.5	-21.6	-46.3	-81.8	-129.1	0	-11.8	-33.3	-65.5	-109.5	-237.4 -426.2
2355	1815	1355	1015	810	680	0	-2.4	-8.2	-17.6	-31.4	-51.5	0	-4.8	-12.8	-25.4	-44.3	-95.5 —
4620	3689	2924	2308	1839	1496	0.7	0	-3.3	-9.6	-19.2	-32.5	2.2	0	-5.2	-13.6	-25.8	-63.2 -121.7
4712	3547	2640	1970	1516	1239	0.8	0	-3.5	-10.3	-20.8	-35.6	2.4	0	-5.6	-14.9	-28.5	-71.5 -140.4

OFFICIAL SCORING SYSTEM FOR NORTH AMERICAN BIG GAME TROPHIES

Records of North American Big Game

BOONE AND CROCKETT CLUB

Old Milwaukee Depot
250 Station Drive
Missoula, MT 59801

Minimum Score:	Awards	All-time
whitetail	160	170
Coues'	100	110

TYPICAL WHITETAIL AND COUES' DEER

Kind of Deer _____

DETAIL OF POINT MEASUREMENT

Abnormal Points	
Right Antler	Left Antler
Subtotals	
Total to E.	

SEE OTHER SIDE FOR INSTRUCTIONS			Column 1 Spread Credit	Column 2 Right Antler	Column 3 Left Antler	Column 4 Difference
A. No. Points on Right Antler		No. Points on Left Antler	✕	✕	✕	
B. Tip to Tip Spread		C. Greatest Spread	✕	✕	✕	✕
D. Inside Spread of Main Beams		(Credit May Equal But Not Exceed Longer Antler)		✕	✕	✕
E. Total of Lengths of Abnormal Points			✕	✕	✕	
F. Length of Main Beam			✕			
G-1. Length of First Point, If Present			✕			
G-2. Length of Second Point			✕			
G-3. Length of Third Point			✕			
G-4. Length of Fourth Point, If Present			✕			
G-5. Length of Fifth Point, If Present			✕			
G-6. Length of Sixth Point, If Present			✕			
G-7. Length of Seventh Point, If Present			✕			
H-1. Circumference at Smallest Place Between Burr and First Point			✕			
H-2. Circumference at Smallest Place Between First and Second Points			✕			
H-3. Circumference at Smallest Place Between Second and Third Points			✕			
H-4. Circumference at Smallest Place Between Third and Fourth Points			✕			
TOTALS						

ADD	Column 1		Exact Locality Where Killed:
	Column 2		Date Killed: By Whom Killed:
	Column 3		Present Owner:
	Subtotal		Owner's Address:
SUBTRACT Column 4			Guide's Name and Address:
FINAL SCORE			Remarks: (Mention Any Abnormalities or Unique Qualities)

I certify that I have measured this trophy on _____ 19 _____

at (address) _____ City _____ State _____
and that these measurements and data are, to the best of my knowledge and belief, made in
accordance with the instructions given.

Witness: _____ Signature: _____

B&C OFFICIAL MEASURER [ ][ ][ ]

I.D. Number

INSTRUCTIONS FOR MEASURING TYPICAL WHITETAIL AND COUES' DEER

All measurements must be made with a 1/4-inch wide flexible steel tape to the nearest one-eighth of an inch. Wherever it is necessary to change direction of measurement, mark a control point and swing tape at this point. (Note: A flexible steel cable can be used to measure points and main beams only.) Enter fractional figures in eighths, without reduction. Official measurements cannot be taken until the antlers have air dried for at least 60 days after the animal was killed.

A. Number of Points on Each Antler: To be counted a point, the projection must be at least one inch long, with the length exceeding width at one inch or more of length. All points are measured from tip of point to nearest edge of beam as illustrated. Beam tip is counted as a point but not measured as a point.

B. Tip to Tip Spread is measured between tips of main beams.

C. Greatest Spread is measured between perpendiculars at a right angle to the center line of the skull at widest part, whether across main beams or points.

D. Inside Spread of Main Beams is measured at a right angle to the center line of the skull at widest point between main beams. Enter this measurement again as the Spread Credit if it is less than or equal to the length of the longer antler; if greater, enter longer antler length for Spread Credit.

E. Total of Lengths of all Abnormal Points: Abnormal Points are those non-typical in location (such as points originating from a point or from bottom or sides of main beam) or extra points beyond the normal pattern of points. Measure in usual manner and enter in appropriate blanks.

F. Length of Main Beam is measured from lowest outside edge of burr over outer curve to the most distant point of what is, or appears to be, the main beam. The point of beginning is that point on the burr where the center line along the outer curve of the beam intersects the burr, then following generally the line of the illustration.

G-1-2-3-4-5-6-7. Length of Normal Points: Normal points project from the top of the main beam. They are measured from nearest edge of main beam over outer curve to tip. Lay the tape along the outer curve of the beam so that the top edge of the tape coincides with the top edge of the beam on both sides of the point to determine the baseline for point measurements. Record point lengths in appropriate blanks.

H-1-2-3-4. Circumferences are taken as detailed for each measurement. If brow point is missing, take H-1 and H-2 at smallest place between burr and G-2. If G-4 is missing, take H-4 halfway between G-3 and tip of main beam.

FAIR CHASE STATEMENT FOR ALL HUNTER-TAKEN TROPHIES

FAIR CHASE, as defined by the Boone and Crockett Club, is the ethical, sportsmanlike and lawful pursuit and taking of any free-ranging wild game animal in a manner that does not give the hunter an improper or unfair advantage over such game animals.

Use of any of the following methods in the taking of game shall be deemed UNFAIR CHASE and unsportsmanlike:

I. Spotting or herding game from the air, followed by landing in its vicinity for the purpose of pursuit and shooting;

II. Herding, pursuing, or shooting game from any motorboat or motor vehicle;

III. Use of electronic devices for attracting, locating, or observing game, or for guiding the hunter to such game;

IV. Hunting game confined by artificial barriers, including escape-proof fenced enclosures, or hunting game transplanted solely for the purpose of commercial shooting;

V. Taking of game in a manner not in full compliance with the game laws or regulations of the federal government or of any state, province, territory, or tribal council on reservations or tribal lands;

VI. Or as may otherwise be deemed unfair or unsportsmanlike by the Executive Committee of the Boone and Crockett Club.

I certify that the trophy scored on this chart was taken in FAIR CHASE as defined above by the Boone and Crockett Club. In signing this statement, I understand that if this entry is found to be fraudulent, it will not be accepted into the Awards program and all of my prior entries are subject to deletion from future editions of *Records of North American Big Game* and future entries may not be accepted.

Date: _____ Signature of Hunter: _____

(Have signature notarized by a Notary Public.)

Copyright © 1993 by Boone and Crockett Club
(Reproduction strictly forbidden without express, written consent)

OFFICIAL SCORING SYSTEM FOR NORTH AMERICAN BIG GAME TROPHIES

Records of North American
Big Game

BOONE AND CROCKETT CLUB

Old Milwaukee Depot
250 Station Drive
Missoula, MT 59801

Minimum Score: Awards All-time
whitetail   185   195
Coues'   105   120

NON-TYPICAL
WHITETAIL AND COUES' DEER

Kind of Deer _____

	Abnormal Points	
	Right Antler	Left Antler
	Subtotals	
	Total to E	

SEE OTHER SIDE FOR INSTRUCTIONS				Column 1	Column 2	Column 3	Column 4
A. No. Points on Right Antler		No. Points on Left Antler		Spread Credit	Right Antler	Left Antler	Difference
B. Tip to Tip Spread		C. Greatest Spread					
D. Inside Spread of Main Beams		(Credit May Equal But Not Exceed Longer Antler)					
E. Total of Lengths of Abnormal Points							
F. Length of Main Beam							
G-1. Length of First Point, If Present							
G-2. Length of Second Point							
G-3. Length of Third Point							
G-4. Length of Fourth Point, If Present							
G-5. Length of Fifth Point, If Present							
G-6. Length of Sixth Point, If Present							
G-7. Length of Seventh Point, If Present							
H-1. Circumference at Smallest Place Between Burr and First Point							
H-2. Circumference at Smallest Place Between First and Second Points							
H-3. Circumference at Smallest Place Between Second and Third Points							
H-4. Circumference at Smallest Place Between Third and Fourth Points							
TOTALS							

ADD	Column 1		Exact Locality Where Killed:
	Column 2		Date Killed: By Whom Killed:
	Column 3		Present Owner:
	Subtotal		Owner's Address:
SUBTRACT Column 4			Guide's Name and Address:
	Subtotal		Remarks: (Mention Any Abnormalities or Unique Qualities)
Add Line E Total			
FINAL SCORE			

I certify that I have measured this trophy on _____ 19 _____
at (Address) _____ City _____ State _____
and that these measurements and data are, to the best of my knowledge and belief, made in
accordance with the instructions given.

Witness: _____ Signature: _____

                                                                  B&C OFFICIAL MEASURER   [ ][ ][ ][ ]

                                                                                                            I.D. Number

INSTRUCTIONS FOR MEASURING NON-TYPICAL WHITETAIL AND COUES' DEER

    All measurements must be made with a 1/4-inch wide flexible steel tape to the nearest one-eighth of an inch. Wherever it is necessary to change direction of measurement, mark a control point and swing tape at this point. (Note: A flexible steel cable can be used to measure points and main beams only.) Enter fractional figures in eighths, without reduction. Official measurements cannot be taken until the antlers have air dried for at least 60 days after the animal was killed.

A.   Number of Points on Each Antler: To be counted a point, the projection must be at least one inch long, with the length exceeding width at one inch or more of length. All points are measured from tip of point to nearest edge of beam as illustrated. Beam tip is counted as a point but not measured as a point.

B.   Tip to Tip Spread is measured between tips of main beams.

C.   Greatest Spread is measured between perpendiculars at a right angle to the center line of the skull at widest part, whether across main beams or points.

D.   Inside Spread of Main Beams is measured at a right angle to the center line of the skull at widest point between main beams. Enter this measurement again as the Spread Credit *if* it is less than or equal to the length of the longer antler; if greater, enter longer antler length for Spread Credit.

E.   Total of Lengths of all Abnormal Points: Abnormal Points are those non-typical in location (such as points originating from a point or from bottom or sides of main beam) or extra points beyond the normal pattern of points. Measure in usual manner and enter in appropriate blanks.

F.   Length of Main Beam is measured from lowest outside edge of burr over outer curve to the most distant point of what is, or appears to be, the main beam. The point of beginning is that point on the burr where the center line along the outer curve of the beam intersects the burr, then following generally the line of the illustration.

G-1-2-3-4-5-6-7.   Length of Normal Points: Normal points project from the top of the main beam. They are measured from nearest edge of main beam over outer curve to tip. Lay the tape along the outer curve of the beam so that the top edge of the tape coincides with the top edge of the beam on both sides of the point to determine the baseline for point measurement. Record point lengths in appropriate blanks.

H-1-2-3-4.   Circumferences are taken as detailed for each measurement. If brow point is missing, take H-1 and H-2 at smallest place between burr and G-2. If G-4 is missing, take H-4 halfway between G-3 and tip of main beam.

FAIR CHASE STATEMENT FOR ALL HUNTER-TAKEN TROPHIES

    FAIR CHASE, as defined by the Boone and Crockett Club, is the ethical, sportsmanlike and lawful pursuit and taking of any free-ranging wild game animal in a manner that does not give the hunter an improper or unfair advantage over such game animals.
    Use of any of the following methods in the taking of game shall be deemed **UNFAIR CHASE** and unsportsmanlike:

    I.   Spotting or herding game from the air, followed by landing in its vicinity for the purpose of pursuit and shooting;

    II.   Herding, pursuing, or shooting game from any motorboat or motor vehicle;

    III.   Use of electronic devices for attracting, locating, or observing game, or for guiding the hunter to such game;

    IV.   Hunting game confined by artificial barriers, including escape-proof fenced enclosures, or hunting game transplanted solely for the purpose of commercial shooting;

    V.   Taking of game in a manner not in full compliance with the game laws or regulations of the federal government or of any state, province, territory, or tribal council on reservations or tribal lands;

    VI.   Or as may otherwise be deemed unfair or unsportsmanlike by the Executive Committee of the Boone and Crockett Club.

I certify that the trophy scored on this chart was taken in FAIR CHASE as defined above by the Boone and Crockett Club. In signing this statement, I understand that if this entry is found to be fraudulent, it will not be accepted into the Awards program and all of my prior entries are subject to deletion from future editions of *Records of North American Big Game* and future entries may not be accepted.

Date: _____ Signature of Hunter: _____
                                                 (Have signature notarized by a Notary Public.)
                    Copyright © 1993 by **Boone and Crockett Club**
         (Reproduction strictly forbidden without express, written consent)

BOWHUNTER'S BIG GAME RECORDS

POPE AND YOUNG CLUB

Under the heading of North American Big Game are included the following with the minimum point score requirements (Boone & Crockett scoring system) as revised May, 1993.

To be eligible for entry into the Pope and Young Records and awards, the trophy must equal or exceed the score listed on the Minimum List and must have been taken by the individual or persons who are entering it, entirely by means of the Bow and Arrow under the Club's Rules of Fair Chase. A Trophy Award Citation will be issued to each qualifying entry.

Cougar taken in any area where a bounty provision of any type is allowed are not eligible for entry in Pope and Young Club Records, or for Record Class Citations.

Southern Boundary of North America to be defined as the Southern Boundary of Mexico.

MINIMUM POINT SCORE REQUIREMENTS

Alaska Brown Bear 20	*Mule Deer, Non-Typical 160 (16)
Black Bear 18	Whitetail Deer, Typical 125
Grizzly Bear 19	Whitetail Deer, Non-Typical 150 (15)
Polar Bear 20	Roosevelt's (Olympic) Elk 225
Bison 100	Yellowstone (Wapiti) Elk 260
*Barren Ground Caribou 325	Yellowstone Elk, Non-Typical 300 (20)
*Central Barren Ground Caribou 300	Rocky Mountain Goat 40
*Mountain Caribou 300	Alaska-Yukon Moose 170
*Quebec-Labrador Caribou 325	Canada Moose 135
*Woodland Caribou 220	Wyoming Moose 115
Cougar 13 8/16	Muskox 90
Columbian Blacktail Deer 90	Pronghorn 64
Columbian Blacktail Deer Non-Typical . . 110 (9)	Bighorn Sheep 140
Sitka Blacktail Deer 75	Dall's (White) Sheep 120
Coues' Deer, Typical 65	Desert Bighorn Sheep 140
Coues' Deer, Non-Typical 75 (7)	Stone's Sheep 120
*Mule Deer, Typical 145	

* Velvet entries are accepted in these categories, the above minimums apply.

Revised May, 1993

BOWHUNTING

BIG GAME

RECORDS

POPE & YOUNG CLUB
P.O. BOX 548
CHATFIELD, MN 55923

FAIR CHASE AFFIDAVIT

To be entered into the Pope & Young Club Records, the animal must meet the minimum scoring requirements, and must be taken in complete compliance with the controlling game laws and the Rules of Fair Chase. The term "Fair Chase" shall not include the taking of animals under the following conditions:

1. Helpless in a trap, deep snow or water, or on ice.
2. From any power vehicle or power boat.
3. While confined behind fences as on game farms, etc.
4. By "Jacklighting" or shining at night.
5. By the use of any tranquilizers or poisons.
6. By the use of any power vehicles or power boat for herding or driving animals, including use of aircraft to land alongside or to communicate with or direct a hunter on the ground.
7. By the use of electronic devices for attracting, locating or pursuing game, or guiding the hunter to such game, or by the use of a bow or arrow to which any electronic device is attached.
8. Any other condition considered by the Board of Directors as unsportsmanlike.

SPECIAL NOTE: For the purpose of the Pope & Young Club, a bow shall be defined as a longbow, recurve bow or compound bow that is hand-held and hand-drawn, and that has no mechanical device to enable the hunter to lock the bow at full or partial draw. Other than energy stored by the drawn bow, no device to propel the arrow will be permitted. A letoff of sixty-five (65) percent on a compound bow is the maximum allowed.

SEARCH & RECOVERY: Was the animal recovered on the same day as hit? YES ☐   NO* ☐
(check one)

*If "NO", give COMPLETE DETAILS
of recovery on back, [COMMENTS], or on a separate sheet.

Falsification of the Fair Chase Affidavit is grounds for dismissal from the Pope & Young Club. Falsification will cause the entry to be rejected, no future entries accepted and all past entries dropped from the Pope & Young Club records for the individual falsifying the affidavit. In addition to the requirements of this affidavit, by submitting this entry the applicant agrees that the sole decision of acceptance of this entry belongs to the Board of Directors and its discretionary decision is in all respects final.

I,_____ attest that my _____
　　　　　　　　　(print)　　　　　　　　　　　　　　　　　　　　　　　　(species)
was taken entirely by the means of BOW & ARROW, and in complete compliance with the controlling game laws and the rules of Fair Chase.

WE THE UNDERSIGNED, DECLARE THAT THE FOREGOING STATEMENTS ARE TRUE TO THE BEST OF OUR KNOWLEDGE AND BELIEF:

_____   _____
　　　　　　Hunter's Signature　　　　　　　　　　　　　　　Date

_____   _____
Witness to verification of bow kill, Signature of witness   (please print name)
(Does not have to be Eye Witness)

_____   _____
　　　Address of witness　　　　　　　　　City　　　　　　State　Zip

THIS FORM MUST BE COMPLETELY FILLED OUT!
REVISED MARCH, 1989

Please complete the following form as it relates to the harvest of this trophy. This information is used by the Pope & Young Club to provide an overall view of the nature of hunts for the various North American big game animals for which we maintain records.

1. SPECIES_____ SEX_____

2. HUNTER INFORMATION: Age_____ Sex_____ Years of bowhunting experience_____

3. HUNT INFORMATION: Guide ☐ ☐ Date of Kill____.____.____
                                             yes no   month day year

   WEATHER CONDITIONS AT TIME OF KILL: Clear ☐ Cloudy ☐ Rain ☐ Snow ☐ Other_____
   Time_____ a.m. p.m. Temperature_____

4. DISTANCE OF SHOT: (if more than one shot, write distance of each arrow in appropriate box)
   #1._____yds. #2._____yds. #3._____yds. #4._____yds.

   For the next four questions, place an X in the space corresponding to each arrow, e.g., if arrow #1 and #3 were both broadside, record your entry as follows: **Broadside**
                                                               EXAMPLE   ☒ ☐ ☒ ☐
                                                                                              1 2 3 4

   ANGLE OF THE SHOT:

Broadside	Rear Quartering	Front Quartering	Rear	Front	Above
☐ ☐ ☐ ☐	☐ ☐ ☐ ☐	☐ ☐ ☐ ☐	☐ ☐ ☐ ☐	☐ ☐ ☐ ☐	☐ ☐ ☐ ☐
1 2 3 4	1 2 3 4	1 2 3 4	1 2 3 4	1 2 3 4	1 2 3 4

   WHERE ARROW STRUCK ANIMAL:

Chest	Paunch	Rump	Leg	Head	Other_____
☐ ☐ ☐ ☐	☐ ☐ ☐ ☐	☐ ☐ ☐ ☐	☐ ☐ ☐ ☐	☐ ☐ ☐ ☐	☐ ☐ ☐ ☐
1 2 3 4	1 2 3 4	1 2 3 4	1 2 3 4	1 2 3 4	1 2 3 4

5. STYLE OF HUNTING: Bait ☐   Stalk ☐   Still ☐   Tree Stand ☐   Ground Blind ☐   Calling ☐   Dogs ☐
   (Stalk - spotting animal first then moving in: Still - locating animal by moving)

6. NUMBER OF MEMBERS IN YOUR HUNTING PARTY WHEN ANIMAL WAS HARVESTED_____

7. NUMBER OF DAYS HUNTING DURING THE SEASON FOR THIS SPECIES_____

8. NUMBER OF ARROWS SHOT DURING THE SEASON AT THIS SPECIES_____

9. NUMBER OF ANIMALS OF THIS SPECIES SEEN DURING THE SEASON_____

10. TYPE OF BOW: Longbow ☐   Recurve ☐   Compound ☐ % Letoff_____ Draw Weight_____ lbs.

    TYPE OF QUIVER: Hip ☐   Back ☐   Bow ☐   Other (specify)_____ Quiver size (number of arrows)____

    TYPE OF BROADHEAD: Fixed blade (no insert) ☐   Fixed blade (with insert) ☐   Replaceable Blade ☐
    Other_____ Number of blades_____

    TYPE OF ARROWS: Wood ☐   Fiberglass ☐   Aluminum ☐   Other (specify)_____ Length_____

11. COMMENTS:

Where They Stand On Hunting:
The Good, The Bad, And The In-Between

The Good

American Archery Council
Archery Manufacturers Organization
Boone & Crockett
Buckmasters
Ducks Unlimited
Foundation for North American Wild Sheep
Fur Takers of America
Game Conservation International
International Association of Fish and Wildlife
International Professional Hunters Association
International Shooting & Hunting Alliance
Izaak Walton League of America
Mzuri Safari
National Association of Hunter Safety Coordinators
National Association of Sporting Goods Wholesalers
National Bowhunter Education Foundation
National Fish & Wildlife Foundation
National Gamebird Association
National Hunters Association
National Institute for Urban Wildlife
National Rifle Association
National Shooting Sports Foundation
National Trappers Association
National Wild Turkey Federation
North American Falconers Association
Outdoor Writers Association of America
Pheasants Forever
Prairie Chicken Foundation
Professional Bowhunters Association
Quail Unlimited
Rocky Mountain Elk Foundation
Ruffed Grouse Society
Safari Club International
Waterfowl USA
Whitetails Unlimited
Wilderness Society
Wildlife Conservation Fund of America
Wildlife Forever
Wildlife Legislative Fund of America
Wildlife Management Institute
Wildlife Society
Putting People First
United Conservation Alliance
North American Hunting Club

The In-Between

National Audubon Society— The national organization has no official anti-hunting stance. However, some state Audubon associations have opposed hunters on certain issues.

National Wildlife Federation— The NWF does not openly endorse hunting. However, it has published materials in which cases favoring hunting were presented. On the other hand, they have also been the plaintiff in court cases which closed many waterfowling areas to lead shot.

Nature Conservancy—Perhaps no other group sits as firmly in the middle on this issue as the Nature Conservancy. It simply refuses to discuss the hunting issue in its literature and takes great pains to maintain its neutral stance.

Sierra Club—The Sierra Club is not an anti-hunting organization. Some hunters have complained in recent years that Sierra's efforts to protect the wilderness have limited hunters' access to hunting land.

The Bad

Actors & Others for Animals
Alliance for Animals
American Humane Association
Animal Emancipation
Animal Legal Defense Fund
Animal Liberation Front
Animal Protection Institute of America
*Animal Rights Network (Animal Agenda)
Animal Welfare Institute
*Committee to Abolish Sport Hunting
Cousteau Society
*Defenders of Wildlife
Doris Day Animal League
EarthFirst!
Elsa Wild Animal Appeal
*Friends of Animals
*Fund for Animals
*Greenpeace
Human/Animal Liberation Front
*Humane Society of the United States
*Hunt Sabateurs
In Defense of Animals
International Fund for Animal Welfare
International Society for Animal Rights
Law Students for Animal Rights
Mobilization for Animals
National Animal Protection Fund
National Humane Education Society
North Shore Animal League
*People for the Ethical Treatment of Animals
Primarily Primates
Progressive Animal Welfare Society
Protect Our Earth's Treasures
*Sea Shepherd Conservation Society
Society for Animal Protective Legislation
Student Animal Rights Coalition
Trans Species Unlimited
United Animal Nations
Wildlife Refuge Reform Coalition
World Society for the Protection of Animals
World Wildlife Fund

*The most active and aggressive anti-hunting groups.

List reprinted with permission from North American Hunter, North American Hunting Club, P.O. Box 3401, Minnetonka, Mn. 55343

HUNTERS CHECKLIST

Preliminary Equipment
- reading glasses
- land maps
- credit cards
- pocket knife

- hunting license
- hunting regs
- presc medicine

- permits
- cash/trav checks
- watch

Hunting Equipment
- gun
- shotgun
- gun cases
- orange vest
- release
- sharpener
- safety belt/harn
- haul string
- camo paint
- blind
- hunting stool

- spare gun
- handgun
- ammunition
- bow
- arm guard
- hot seat
- climbing steps
- rattling antlers
- scents/lures
- pruning tool
- scope cover

- small bore rifle
- gun slings
- spare ammo
- arrows
- hunting knife
- tree stand
- climbing belt
- grunt/game calls
- decoys
- rubber gloves

Hunting Accessories
- shell holder
- butcher knife
- binoculars
- window mount
- compass
- shooting glasses
- ear plugs
- spare bow
- targets
- back lic holder

- spare clips
- bone saw
- spotting scope
- drag rope
- pen light
- ramrod
- gun cleaning kit
- archery equip
- back pack
- gut hook knife

- spare knife
- liver bag
- tripod
- wind dir tester
- range finder
- ballistic chart
- spare bow string
- spare arrows/case
- fanny pack

Clothes
- travel clothes
- hunt hat
- balaclava
- scarf
- u-shirt
- hooded swtshirt
- wool pants
- camp pants
- union suit
- polyprop socks
- rubber boots
- spare liners
- rain gear
- camo coveralls

- travel boots
- hunt cap
- winter mask
- gloves-2 pr
- wool shirts
- sweaters
- brush pants
- u-wear
- suspenders
- cotton socks
- leather boots
- hunting coat
- bib overalls
- bandanna

- travel coat/hat
- orange hat
- mesh face mask
- mittens
- insul shirts(2)
- down vest
- camo pants
- insul u-wear-2
- wool socks-3pr
- pac boots
- hiking boots
- hunter orange
- insul coveralls
- laundry bag

Survival Gear
- [ ] first aid kit
- [ ] matches
- [ ] long burn candle
- [ ] walkie-talkie
- [ ] trail mix
- [ ] snake bite kit
- [ ] lip protection
- [ ] ace bandages
- [ ] water pur tablets
- [ ] butane lighter
- [ ] magnifying glass
- [ ] bota/canteen
- [ ] flares
- [ ] insect repellent
- [ ] surveyors tape
- [ ] space blanket
- [ ] spare compass
- [ ] emerg fire starter
- [ ] flashlight
- [ ] aspirin
- [ ] signal mirror
- [ ] hand warmer
- [ ] metal whistle
- [ ] _____
- [ ] _____

Travel/camp tools and equipment
- [ ] toilet kit
- [ ] road maps
- [ ] note pad
- [ ] lantern
- [ ] safety matches
- [ ] come-a-long
- [ ] jumper cables
- [ ] rope
- [ ] axe/saw
- [ ] sleeping bag
- [ ] ground tarp
- [ ] cot
- [ ] thermometer
- [ ] scent shield
- [ ] cups
- [ ] paper towels
- [ ] cooking utensils
- [ ] thermos
- [ ] water storage
- [ ] brillo pads
- [ ] CB radio
- [ ] spare knife sharp
- [ ] pack board
- [ ] _____
- [ ] _____
- [ ] alarm clock
- [ ] triptik
- [ ] pencils/pens
- [ ] spare mantles
- [ ] port-a-potty
- [ ] game hoist
- [ ] tire chains
- [ ] nylon cord
- [ ] splitting maul
- [ ] pillow
- [ ] plastic tarp
- [ ] air mattress
- [ ] washcloth/towel
- [ ] heater
- [ ] pots/pans/lids
- [ ] toilet paper
- [ ] can opener
- [ ] corkscrew
- [ ] dish soap
- [ ] boot dressing
- [ ] playing cards
- [ ] game bags
- [ ] work gloves
- [ ] _____
- [ ] _____
- [ ] sunglasses
- [ ] diary/log book
- [ ] spotlight
- [ ] white gas/propane
- [ ] shovel
- [ ] tow chain
- [ ] gasoline can
- [ ] camp seats
- [ ] fire grate
- [ ] blankets
- [ ] tent
- [ ] air pump
- [ ] soap/case
- [ ] cook stove
- [ ] plates/dishes
- [ ] eating utensils
- [ ] coffee pot
- [ ] storage cooler
- [ ] dishcloth/towel
- [ ] radio
- [ ] hand tools
- [ ] garbage bags
- [ ] television
- [ ] _____
- [ ] _____

Miscellaneous Items
- [ ] gifts for host
- [ ] pepto bismol
- [ ] candy bars
- [ ] tobacco products
- [ ] flash attachment
- [ ] needle/thread
- [ ] fingernl scissors
- [ ] camo tape
- [ ] address book
- [ ] baking soda
- [ ] spare veh keys
- [ ] _____
- [ ] _____
- [ ] _____
- [ ] vitamins
- [ ] chewing gum
- [ ] hard candies
- [ ] camera
- [ ] video camera
- [ ] safety pins
- [ ] electric tape
- [ ] ziploc bags
- [ ] spare batteries
- [ ] food item list
- [ ] kitchen sink
- [ ] _____
- [ ] _____
- [ ] _____
- [ ] antacid
- [ ] snacks
- [ ] juice
- [ ] film
- [ ] magazines
- [ ] tweezers
- [ ] duct tape
- [ ] tinfoil
- [ ] spare read glasses
- [ ] padlock
- [ ] _____
- [ ] _____
- [ ] _____

THE END!

Photo by Ted Rose